HOLT

AN ILLUSTRATED HISTORY
Volume I 1900-1920s

by

Keith Entwistle

with

maps and illustrations

by

Geraldine Frances

Published by

BRICK KILN BOOKS
Watch Oak

Copyright © 2004 Keith Entwistle

Illustrations copyright © 2004 Geraldine Frances

First published in Great Britain in 2004

by

ISBN: 0-9549045-0-8

Typeset in Univers and Hiroshige
by Claire Knight

Printed and bound in Great Britain
by Broadgate Printers, Aylsham

Contents

Holt counted just over 400 households in 1900, with a population of 1854.
Thirty years later, there was a slight overall increase to 1940 persons.

Introduction

The Holt History Project came into being with two aims in view. The first was to start the process of creating a Holt archive, so that there may be a permanent resource on the town's history. Second, we have wanted to publish our findings in the form of a book, or books, which I undertook to write and publish on the Project's behalf.

Fifteen months later... Here we are in print with the first volume! We started by making a general appeal, through the press, for materials of all kinds – documents, photographs, diaries, newspaper cuttings, family archives. Then, in October 2003, we held a two-day History Roadshow in the Church Hall, an event which proved a major success, both in terms of materials brought in, and in the number of leads to follow up. The whole process acquires the nature of hunt, genteel perhaps in character, but we display an equivalent zeal in pursuit of our quarry! Six months later we held our Exhibition in Picturecraft, the response to which has kept us flying ever since. And so the book.

It is arranged into nine chapters, eight of which take us on a tour through the town as it was in the first three decades of the twentieth century. We have period photos depicting nearly every building in the main parts of the town, and we take time absorbing aspects of daily life particular to each; we learn about different customs, personalities and pursuits. The tour is enlivened by a series of eight charming pictorial maps, drawn by Geraldine Frances, which highlight the key features along the way. The one chapter which is not topographically based deals with the period of the First World War taken as a whole. There will be some surprises!

In compiling a book of this nature, I like to use first-hand testimony wherever possible. This comes in two forms – the written and the spoken. As regards the former, we are very fortunate to have had the works of Jane Hales to hand. As many of you know, she was born in the town and lived her whole life here, fitting her ninety-plus years entirely within the span of the twentieth century. Further notable written sources came to light, too. First to hand was the fascinating *A Family Remembers*, a memoir of the nine children of the Revd HA King, Rector of Holt 1909-1947. A few months later I was thrilled to have access to the recollections of a Gresham's housemaster, Dallas Wynne Wilson, resident in Old School House for many years. His memories make a sensational contribution to our knowledge of the town during the First World War.

The recorded conversation is the other indispensable source, placed throughout the text under the title – A Holt Childhood.

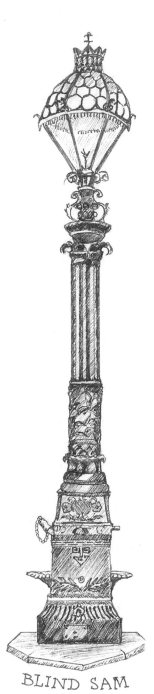

BLIND SAM

In transcribing these conversations, my aim has been to retain the vivid qualities – and the pure unpredictability – of spoken recollection. At the same time I am aware that my 'audience' is reading, not listening! Conversations recalling the past tend to go from 'high' to 'low' to 'high' again, recalling moments, people, experiences which retain significance after seventy or eighty years. A further delight of these conversations is the quality brought in terms of atmosphere and texture of those days.

We come to the photography. The visual record of Holt over the twentieth century is incredibly rich; Archie Checkley recognised this from an early age and in the course of his life he collected photographs and Holt memorabilia of all kinds. It is our good fortune that his albums are now preserved in the Norfolk Record Office. I should add that Archie was not alone in his zeal and other private collectors have been enormously generous in granting access to their material.

Throughout the project my practice has been first to look and listen, then to think and link. I have been aware from the outset that the last full-scale book on Holt was written in 1908. There have been specialist publications which have proved invaluable in providing information in their field of study, but Holt as town has not been their focus. My aim therefore has been to establish a baseline, and throughout I've posed a very fundamental, but essential, question: What was Holt actually like in the early years of the twentieth century? My attempt to answer that lies in the tour of the town you are about to undertake. There are disadvantages of any scheme of organisation of material in a book of this kind. One method is to have an arrangement of topics – Education, Sport, Administration, Church, Chapel, Clubs, Health, Societies – and the like. However, I soon came to the conclusion that if a forge can be next to a chapel in the street, it can be neighbourly when it comes to print and pictures on the page! Moreover, if I had decided to put everything in relation to Holt schools in one block, just think how long a chapter that would be!

Finally, I should like to thank everybody who has contributed to the creation of this volume. Our Acknowledgments page, which you will find at the end of the book, features a very long list of participants – it has truly been a team enterprise. However, responsibility for the final text and selection of image has to rest with me.

The time for your visit to the Holt of the early twentieth century has now come.

Welcome!

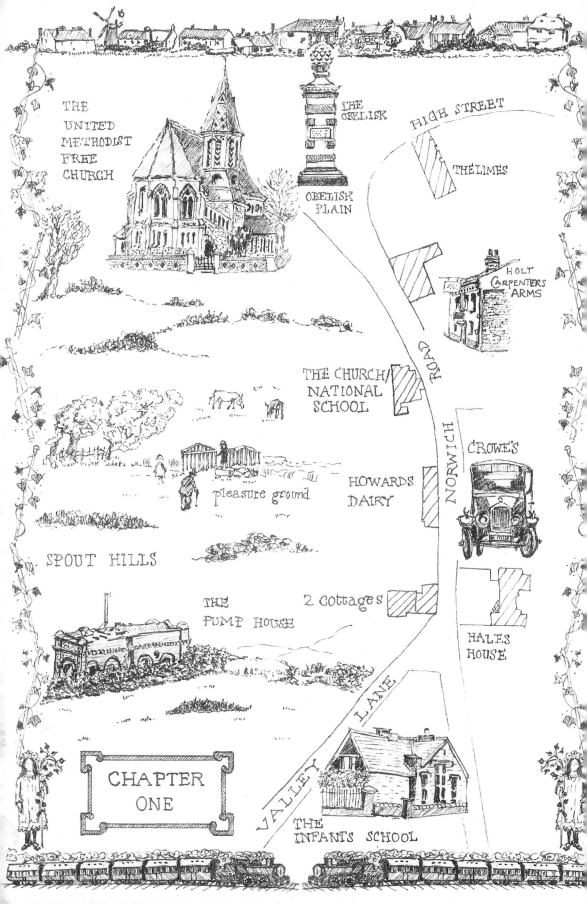

THE UNITED METHODIST FREE CHURCH

THE OBELISK

OBELISK PLAIN

HIGH STREET

THE LIMES

HOLT CARPENTERS ARMS

ROAD

THE CHURCH/NATIONAL SCHOOL

NORWICH

CROWE'S

pleasure ground

HOWARDS DAIRY

SPOUT HILLS

THE PUMP HOUSE

2 Cottages

HALES HOUSE

VALLEY LANE

CHAPTER ONE

THE INFANTS SCHOOL

Chapter 1

Spout Hills

William White's History, Gazetteer and Directory of Norfolk, 1883

On Spout common, on the south-west side of the town, a copious spring issues out of the gravel hill, and affords an ample supply of pure soft water, which is carried in carts to the town, where there are also three public pumps. The spring head is walled round, and is visited by many as a natural curiosity, and for the prospect of enjoying the fine prospect which it commands over the romantic valley of the Glaven.

We start in the west and we start with water. In our current age we live in ignorance of the precise origin of our water, but for centuries the people of Holt knew exactly where their water gushed – the hills. It flowed perpetually from a natural spring they'd christened the Spout. The very name reveals their confidence in its power – not the Dribble, not the Spring, but the Spout! In the chapter on Holt in her book *The East Wind*, Jane Hales quotes an early edict:

> The said place called the Spouts shall for ever hereafter continue to be used for the purpose of supplying the inhabitants of the said parish of Holt with Water... for ever hereafter to be used by the persons having the Right of Common thereon as a common pasture and in such manner as they have been accustomed to use the same, but not for the purpose of cutting fuel.

But as this extract makes clear, the Hills were more than the source of water – they were common land set aside to the townspeople for grazing, a right instituted in the Enclosure Act of 1810. And more than this, they were available for recreation. The Parish Council of the Parish of Holt published these byelaws on February 1st, 1898:

Byelaws with respect to a Pleasure Ground

Throughout these byelaws the expression *The Council* means the Parish Council of the Parish of Holt; and the expression *The Pleasure Ground* means the pleasure ground known as Spout Hills.

Very formal and very clear – the communal powers defined the Hills as a *pleasure ground* – what a wonderful term! – for relaxation and play. For the town's children, the Hills were a 'wonderland'. Every current resident of Holt to grow up in the first half of the twentieth century talks of the many hours spent in careless enjoyment on the hills. One of these is Earle Kirby, who grew up off New Street, from where a footpath cuts across to the hills.

Earle Kirby "The actual hill was divided into two sections cut across by the Fakenham road. I as a boy who lived on the Fairstead used to play mainly on what was termed the Little Hills. On the other side of the road, which was really what they called 'distant territory for us children' was the larger part of the hills which was called the Big Hills, and here there was the Spout, the water which ran out of the side of the hill. At the bottom end in the valley was the old Pumping Station, which used to pump the water up to the tower in the middle of Holt; this was run by a man called Arnold Burrell. We used to start by

playing on the Little Hills, but we always wanted to go across to the Big Hills, and my parents used to say, "Don't you cross that road, it's a very dangerous road!" but we used to get across somehow! There was a lovely little stream which ran down from the Spout, through the hills, through the Old Rectory at the bottom of the hill and down into Letheringsett, and we used to sail little paper boats down there and have a whale of a time in there, we really did, it was a lovely old place. The whole area of the Hills is so compact as you look at it today, but for us as children it was a massive place, it was a wonderland. We used to play all round the pumping-station, make bridges, dam the little stream…"

Damming the little stream sounds an innocent enough pastime – but you may be sure, there was a sinister motive! Earle talks of that stream running through the Rectory garden and down into Letheringsett. Well, the net effect of the damming operation higher up caused something of a nuisance to those resident in the Rectory. Henry Hobart's home was on Fish Hill, but his days were spent on the hills.

Henry Hobart "When the river was there – 'cos all the pubs used to have the water from there, you know, we used to dam the river up near the waterworks, especially those days when the parson was having a party, we used to flood the lawn, you know, it was a wicked thing to do! We did that once or twice."

Not only the boys.

Mabel Gotts "We spent our life on the Spout Hills, that was our playground, we loved it. When Good Friday came, we'd go to get the violets, primroses, we used to go in Runton Poor, a wood along the railway line, that was the done thing that was, to get these flowers for our mothers. And then once a year, the Salvation Army, they were a great big lot then, and they really did play, and there used to be a rally, every year. We'd get dressed up, sit about and sing all the hymns. I know one friend, who lived up the Norwich Road, next to the Carpenters Arms yard, every night she had to bring a great big basket with her, and before we went home, we went running round the hills to fill it with sticks for her to take home to her mother, because she was afraid to go home without them. We used to take our tea on there, in summer we'd be on there till nine o'clock. We used to make great big banks, right near the waterworks there, and when we let that go, that would go into poor old parson King's garden, that would flood it! Gardener Gotts used to come after us, but it didn't make any difference, we used to do it all the same!"

Mabel gives further illustrations of the opportunities for play offered by the hills.

Mabel Gotts "We used to play with tops on the Obelisk, then we would go on the Hills and get old pieces of cardboard, when that was dry, slide down on the cardboard. When we were young we used to play concerts, when there was a lot of broom on the hills, we'd make a stage, dress ourselves up with daisies. When I was about seven we said we'd have a fairy concert, and we trimmed ourselves up with daisies all round our heads, and my mother had bought me a new petticoat, and that had got blue silk ribbon trimmed round the neck. Well, of course, I thought that was marvellous, so I took my dress off. There was always gorse and broom bushes, which were all in flower. Now there was a boy by the name of Anthony who was a loner, and who lived up the Carpenters Arms yard. This Anthony had a very gruff voice. We didn't know he was there. I was the first one to come out, I sang 'I am a little fairy!' and this gruff voice said, 'And I'm a blooming elbe!' – there he was behind the bush, he couldn't say 'elf'!"

Beating the bounds

Jane Hales makes this observation in *Three Centuries of Holt:* This was a necessity before the days of accurate surveys, and was done annually, or every three years, at Rogation time. At a Vestry meeting in 1871, it was agreed to walk the bounds on May 16th starting from the Glebe Barn, on the Letheringsett Road, at 10am. The Assistant Overseer was bidden to inform the neighbouring parish officers to meet them at the following times: Letheringsett, 10am and 3.30pm; Cley, 10.30am, Salthouse, 10.45am, Kelling, 10.45; Bodham,

11.30am, Hempstead, 12 noon; Edgefield, 2pm, Hunworth, 2.45pm; Thornage, 3pm.

Here is Rhoda Bunn's caption to this photograph in her book, *Holt and District*. Schoolgirls from the old Church School in Norwich Road dressed for performing the custom of 'Beating the Bounds'; an ancient ritual which involved going round the parish boundaries tapping the hedgerows and earth with sticks. The custom was supposed to ensure the fertility of the soil and a good harvest. May Day was believed to be the date for this event.

THE
PUMP HOUSE

The Pump House

This solid and squat brick building, constructed of red brick, designed both to fit its function and to please the eye, housed the pumps that brought water to the town between 1885 and its demolition in the mid-fifties. As we have seen, the Spout had been the source of water for generations, water-carts plying between the Hills and the streets. Then the Erpingham Rural Sanitary Authority saw the role that a deep bore and mechanical pumps could play in supplying the town. The fuel needed to work the machinery – gas – was available nearby, Shirehall Plain could easily accommodate a water-tower, the engineers were sure the job could be done – and so it was.

In his days as an apprentice with CT Bakers, who had the maintenance contract on the waterworks, John Jarvis saw its day-by-day operation. Here he gives us a tour of the Pump House.

John Jarvis "There was one entrance to the building, at the town end, blocked-off windows along the side. The inside was lit by skylight by day, otherwise by gas-light. Stepping through the double doors, you saw two huge engines, one larger than the other, in a line before you; each had a massive flywheel, and was raised on a concrete plinth, to which it was bolted down. To your right was the well, about six feet in diameter, with a steel lining. This had a depth of about ninety feet, down to a platform. To climb down, there was a steel ladder, bolted to the side. The platform was not the bottom of the well as such; it was possible to open it up and descend further into the bore – to a total depth of 120 to 130 feet. The pump shafts consisted of steel rods, about an inch and a quarter in diameter, in sections, each about ten feet in length; these were inserted into sleeves which formed joints at intervals. The larger engine was used to draw water from the full depth of the bore, the smaller one from the well. The huge pressure to which the shafts were subject caused the rods to break from time to time. When this happened, the fractured rod had to be removed from the sleeve at either end, then raised by block and tackle. After that, its considerable weight was borne on the shoulders of two men, who carried it through the town to the forge in Bakers premises, where it was mended in the forge. The operation to remove or insert the rods was fraught with danger. Men were stationed on wooden bearers to perform the work, undertaken to the overwhelming background noise of rushing water. A system of signalling had to be devised to effect communication. Another major problem was the shortage of time available – with the pumps out of action, the town was running out of water, and the water levels were rising in the well."

oking back towards the
wn, with the footpath
:ess to Spout Hills top
ht. The wall is to the
rden of Hill House, home
Dr Skrimshire and his
ter Amy. The thought of
those apples behind was
tempting for Henry
bart! See Chapter Five.

Dora Hills "I can remember my dad saying, when he was coming out of school, the people at the King's Head used to ask them to go on there and get them some jugs of water 'cos he wanted it to put in the whiskey. My dad said they used to fight over who used to go down and get it, 'cos they used to get tuppence or something."

Mabel Gotts "One old lady was Mrs Sargent, who never missed, twice a day, used to fill her jugs up, twice a day, she'd come morning, come afternoon."

Further Fun

Other reflections on the hills – and other activities.

Earle Kirby "It was wonderfully kept in those days, and the reason for this was that people in Holt had animal grazing rights, they kept ponies and goats, which they kept tethered – they had to do that – these used to keep the grass immaculate. My parents loved going over there and have a picnic, we'd play n the pond and the stream. And in those days we bird-nested, it was a great hobby, they don't allow it these days. We had strict rules, you were never allowed to take more than one egg from a nest. We were very interested in the wild life."

Henry Hobart "On Holt Hills when I was a kid, there were five horses belonging to Baldry, two belonging to Gant, one other horse and one goat. There was never any sheep on there, never any cattle, but always seven or eight horses on there. The place was wild, no part of it was shut off, it was full of birds, every boy used to go bird-nesting, my age, but the point was we always used to go early, when we took eggs, it was always the first round; most birds have a second round. I had seventy or eighty different sorts, all collected by myself."

Earle Kirby "We used to go about in groups, we were very strong followers of Robin Hood. We'd make bows and arrows, we'd go into the top wood, the Plantin, at the far end of the Little Hills. We used to go in there cut hazel, for bows and the small ones for arrows."

Children pose for the lens of the itinerant photographer, working for one of the postcard companies, who came to Holt to photograph key sites in town (about 1905). Note the gentleman in the panama hat. He liked to be in the picture too!

The Hills provided space for informal sporting encounters, too.

Henry Hobart "Every Sunday morning when I was young there used to be twenty or thirty teenagers collect on the Big Hills, on the top there behind the gasworks – there were no bushes then, we used to play football, without fail. Another thing I used to be caddy for Ronald Deterding, when he used to go with the Miss Reids from the High Street, they used to play golf starting near the gasworks and they used to go right across and up to the railway line. The Reids lived in one of the houses at the bottom end of the town."

And in winter, sledging!

Edith Pointin "We children in Holt had a lovely childhood as we had the Little Hills and Big Hills to play on. In the summer there were always the streams and pond to paddle in. We always took an old cup to have a drink out of the spout that came from a spring underneath a mound nearby. We took packed teas in the summer and in winter, when there was snow, we took our sledges and had great times going down the Hills. The Gresham schoolboys would come, too, with their posh sledges whilst we only had homemade ones."

ry of the Hills

Tory of the Hills

One elderly man made the Hills his home.

Earle Kirby "Of course, we were told by our parents to be careful, but there was an old vagrant gentleman who used to live on the Hills, he used to really look after all us children, he didn't have any home, he slept out rough; I believe he used to sleep in the cokehouse, where they used to make the coke in the gasworks. An old friend of mine Billy Nelson told me he used to give him some of his food and he used to sleep on a pile of sacks by the ovens, which was lovely and warm. He was known as 'Tory of the Hills', that was his name."

Edith Pointin "I only remember one man who didn't work and had no home. His name was George Abraham, but was known as Tory. He would hold the gentlemen's horses for one pence or two pence. I don't know how he lived. I know Mother would give him a bag of cakes and in the summer he slept on the Hills."

He seems to have both befriended the children and helped the adults.

Henry Hobart "Tory lived on the Hills and he acted as a guard, because in those days it was against the law to play cards for money. Half a dozen chaps from Holt used go on there and play cards and Tory used to patrol looking for police, you see. He was always about up there."

Mabel Gotts "Tory Abrahams used to sleep in the gasworks, he was a nice old man, from a good family, kept himself beautifully clean, wash his clothes on the Hills, and hang them out on the bushes to dry – he wouldn't hurt a fly. He was always kind to us children, none of us were frightened of him. When the men played pitch-halfpenny on the Hills, they used to go right over the common to do that, so the police wouldn't see them, and Tory acted as lookout. The men used to play quoits down on that bottom part, we'd watch them do that. There used to be a place where the heat came out, so we'd dry our socks, but Mum always knew, because they would be dirty."

The Crowe family lived nearby in the Norwich Road.

Dora Hills "Old Tory lived up the yard where we lived, he lived in the stable – he'd evidently been in the war, he was ever such a tall, clean man, and he'd evidently come on to hard times, my grand-parents gave him a home up there, he lived in the stables, they always used to make sure he had plenty of food. He'd go on the Holt Hills and he'd wash on the Holt Hills; he used to wash his thick clothes out in the stream, or in the pond, and dry them on the Hills, he was a very fussy old gentleman. He used to go into the Carpenters Arms, and the Gants were ever so kind to him; he was well cared for. One day he had toothache, and he put a piece of string round it and pulled it out! He took very ill, and they took him to what we called the workhouse in those days, the workhouse at West Beckham, and he died there; he had a pauper's funeral. His name was George Abram. Somebody said he had a sister in Cromer."

Valley Lane

This was the original road to Thornage, before the building of the railway blocked it over, requiring the present road to be cut through. Valley Farm lies down a track off this lane. Geoffrey Shaw, music master at Gresham's in the early years of the century, lived here. His son, Sebastian, became a prominent Shakespearian actor. Near the junction with Norwich Road was the yard to CT Bakers, and on the corner stood these two cottages.

These cottages were demolished in the early seventies to widen the road. Note the gas-lamp on the right. Gus Holt made a twice-daily round of the town, to light at night and extinguish in the morning. He cycled with ladders on his shoulder!

Norwich Road

Perhaps Norwich Road is the thoroughfare which has changed in character more than any other since the bypass was routed this way in the nineteen eighties. The photos in this section show how it was for much of the twentieth century, when the traveller from Norwich would cross the railway line over a bridge at the site of the present roundabout, then continue on the new stretch of road, bordered on the right by a high brick wall, the original parts of which were built in 1866. This stretch only came into being as a result of the laying of the railway line in the 1880s. Following that, the first major change was the building of the Infants School, which opened in 1910. From there until Obelisk Plain, Norwich Road continued as a narrow street with buildings on the left up to the very edge of the roadway. These included the Church School (known also as the National School), of which no photo has ever come to light, despite constant research and repeated appeals!

Sturdy infants in fine clothes.

The Infants School

The new Infants School opened on 23rd May 1910, with Miss Maggie Elizabeth Chalker as Head Mistress. Up to this point, Holt children had been educated at either the British (later the Board) School in New Street (originally a Methodist foundation) or the Church School in Norwich Road (an Anglican foundation). In 1903 responsibility for education passed to the County Council, and the idea of creating a separate school for infants was first mentioned in the joint minute-book in October 1907. Various possible sites were considered, including on land behind the existing Church School, and a site called Horn Pits. On the 25 inch 1906 Ordnance map this is identified as being on the high land on the northern side of Letheringsett Hill – otherwise known as the Little Hills. Eventually a third site was offered by the Oddy family, and selected by the managers. 'We recommend the Committee to accept Mr DC Oddy's offer to sell for £300 his triangular meadow Number 145 on the 25inch Ordnance map, bounded by the Norwich Road and by the railway. Mr Oddy stipulates that we should widen the Norwich Road at this point. This seems to us most reasonable. The eight managers who were present unanimously agreed that on public grounds this was the best site available, although it was understood that on personal grounds it was inconvenient to one of them.' In addition to Miss Chalker, there were the following staff: Miss Mildred Mary Thurlow, Miss Elizabeth Wright, and Miss Delia Millicent Roy Bunkell, Monitress.

Maggie Chalker was appointed as first headmistress of the Infants School from 1910 to 1916. Her qualified assistant was Mildred Thurlow, later succeeded by Miss Chapman. The much-loved and long-serving Delia Bunkell began her career as uncertificated teacher in May 1912, followed in April 1917 by Helen Ramm who was appointed by the new head, Dorothy Jackson, and who would later transfer to the Church School. Miss Bunkell would frequently deputise in the Head's absence, through to the 1920s when Miss Grace Chapman from Aylsham took over the headship

The Hales Family

If we were to pursue Radford's adage 'the parish is a nation in miniature', then the Hales family is a strong contender for the municipal aristocracy! For much of the second half of the twentieth century, indeed, Jane Hales was, in the wider county, virtually synonymous with Holt; this arose both through her work with the Red Cross, and from her writing, much of which drew from her deep knowledge of Norfolk and rural life. Both these areas of activity stem from a family tradition; as regards medicine, her father, Dr Robert Hales, (known in the town as Dr Bob) inherited the medical practice from his father, operating (in all senses of the word!) from the family house in Norwich Street. In connection with her life-long interest in all things Norfolk, this was evidently a topic much explored within the family, as this extract from a memoir written by WH Marcon shortly after the death of Doctor Hales (in 1931) makes clear: 'Dr Bob had a profound knowledge of countryside folk. His experiences of their characteristics, customs, sayings, doings, etc have often been told to me.'

Dr Robert Hales

Dr Hales practised medicine in the town all his adult life. He was born in 1853, and continued working until a few years before his death in 1931. He was married to Alice, and they had four children, Henry, Frances, Robert and Jane – born in 1904, nine years after Robert. Dr Hales was very active in the town in other capacities, too. WH Marcon writes, 'In politics he was an ardent Conservative, and a prominent member of the North Norfolk Conservative Association. Up to his death he was a member of the Executive Committee, and President of the Holt and District branch of the Association. His last appearance on a political platform was in July of last year when Lord Beaverbrook spoke in Holt Market Place on behalf of Mr TA Cook.' In addition to his political activities, he is listed in the 1911 Almanack as being on the council of St Andrews Church, and a Manager of both the Church School, Norwich Road, and the Council School, New Street. He is also listed as the Public Vaccinator and Certifying Factory Surgeon.

In her last book *Ninety Years in One House*, written in 1991, Jane Hales describes the daily routine of her doctor father.

> I saw little of my father when I was a young child, as after his rounds of patients he used to have his tea sitting alone in the library, in winter before a large fire, with his hands turned up to the flames and his dogs on the rug. By dinner-time I was in bed, and I did not come down to the meal until I was sixteen.
>
> In after years I heard of what went on in the surgery from

those who attended there. It was a fair-sized room with a table near the window, a counter fitted with a bench and rows of shelves filled with bottles. The room was heated by an open fire, a couple of dogs before it, and near the corner a white cockatoo with a yellow plume perched in a cage. When the bird screamed, William Dady, the dispenser, would poke it with the wooden part of a pen. Then there was a small consulting-room used occasionally for special patients.

acon, the coachman, nd the gig.

Patients came from far and wide, especially on Friday, market day. They tied their donkeys or ponies, which had drawn their carts to the wall of the back drive, or leaned their bicycles there. Some arrived on foot. My father, in a dressing-gown after his bath, sat at the table listening to the patients' ailments, and in between times, accusing Dady of all and sundry misdemeanours. Dady would get redder in the face, and the line of patients would snigger and laugh out loud, knowing it untrue but thinking it a joke. So the entertainment continued till most of the patients left feeling much better from the laughter than they were likely to feel from a bottle of physic. There was no having to go to a chemist in those days, all was done by the dispenser, even to the making of pills.

When the surgery was nearly empty, my father would get up and go into the stable, and cut firewood with a strange-looking Swiss saw. Doctor Dady, as the dispenser was called, prescribed for the patients that remained, giving them mostly bottles of 'White Mixture'. He also made 'Physics'. Some liquid was poured in a glass, and a powder added, and it bubbled up and tasted nice, and was said to cure any headache or other small ailment. Anyhow, it did no harm.

After dressing, my father would either go on his rounds in gig or dog-cart with the coachman, Alfred Bacon, driving, or walk up Holt High Street with his ivory-headed stick and trail of dogs. He would shout greetings to people on the other side of the street, and bellow what he thought was wrong and what he thought of somebody. Two of his special bugbears were Norwich City Football Club, because it was professional sport, and the Gresham's school, then called the Grammar School, which he thought had usurped local boys' privileges. Strangers would ask sometimes why he was not had up for slander, to be told, "That's only Doctor Bob."

Jane Hales as a child

Bacon, the coachman, whom we often called 'Father', had been with my grandfather, and was a kind but superior person. He was an expert horseman, and my father would have nothing but thoroughbreds. Once I made him quite angry by dropping a sack of straw on his bent back through the granary trap-door. When I was very young I slept in my father's dressing-room by a little window overlooking the yard. In the morning I watched Bacon washing the carriages, and making the shh-shh noise common to coachmen. There was the gig with solid rubber fitted on the wheels, the dog-cart, the Victoria, which was a low, curved-shape open carriage, the Brougham which was closed, and the red sledge for snow. It had one long seat and the coachman was perched behind on a small one and held the reins over the passengers' heads.

Jane writes this appreciation of her mother:

I was devoted to my mother. She was a knowledgeable botanist and had a passion for flowers, and her one ambition in life, as far as I am aware, was to have a garden with a stream running through it. This she never got, though we made her a small pool... Incidentally, she was one of the three Alices to whom Lewis Carroll dedicated Alice in Wonderland... On a Sunday, my mother would return from church, go straight into the greenhouse, look round at the plants and leave her gloves and prayer book there. She would then wander in the garden pulling out weeds, and getting hot, would leave some of her nether garments in the potting shed drawer, where maybe they were found by the gardener next morning. And she would not go indoors until the gong for lunch had sounded several times.

Alice Hales

Here follows an 'Appreciation by an Old Friend', which appeared in the press shortly after the death of Doctor Robert Hales. I quote it in full, as it gives incidental detail which we would otherwise miss, but the word 'cheery', used four times in all, raises a critical hackle:

So 'Doctor Bob' has passed over; laid in his resting place on Wednesday of last week. Holt somehow does not seem quite the same, as one by one the old faces cease to be seen, and cheery greetings are no more. It is many years now since I first saw the doctor; in my mind's eye I see him now, perched high up in his gig, the reins in the hands of Bacon, a figure as well known in the countryside of North Norfolk as was his master. It was always of interest to meet 'Dr Bob'. He generally had some fresh yarn to relate, or a question to ask – of which he generally already knew the answer – but wanted to see what you would say. His cheery voice could be heard from one end of Holt Market Place to the other, and strangers must have sometimes wondered as to whether shouting greetings over a space of fifty yards or so was a usual custom in Norfolk.

And then those cheery bowls parties on that delightful lawn of his 'neath the shade of age-old trees; what happy afternoons they were, for he delighted in entertaining his friends, and seeing those around him enjoying themselves. Often have I been one of a party of cheery souls, many of whom, alas, like 'Dr Bob', have thrown their last wood. A gruff manner hid a golden heart. Like his father he often forgot to send in his bills; money had little attraction for him if it came from the poor.

Nobody, with perhaps the exception of the late Mr Walter Rye, had a greater store of Norfolk knowledge – of men, their sayings and doings, their foibles and fancies – than had Hales of Holt. And the criticism could be biting at times, especially if the person happened to be of a different political colour to the worthy doctor. Not quite so much in the public eye of late years, yet we shall miss you greatly, 'Dr Bob'; may the soil rest lightly on your ashes, and memory like the grass be ever green. Goodbye.

The Crowe Family

The Crowe family are mentioned as one of the carriers in the town in the 1845 edition of Whites Directory. In this century, Frederick Crowe (father to fourteen children) passed the business first to son Reggie, who sadly was to die in a freak accident while working on a vehicle in the workshops, and then to Alfred. There are many memories of journeys with Alfred in a variety of vehicles, from carts and wagonettes, to cars, charabancs and Belsize taxis. One unusual aspect of the journey to which passengers grew accustomed was the basket of homing pigeons in the boot. In the course of this volume we learn of the very strong tradition in Holt of pigeon-racing, and Alfred was one of the principal participants. He kept his birds in a loft behind the house, and they accompanied him to many of his business destinations. Once there, he would release them for a training flight back to base. His daughter Dora Hills (born 1923) has a scrapbook of photos of him with prize birds, and newspaper cuttings which record his successes. Dora has a sharp memory for many features of her early childhood.

eg Crowe, at your service! Hood extra.

A 'real native' of Holt

Jane Hales, the Crowe's neighbour in Norwich Road, wrote this letter to the Eastern Daily Press, in appreciation of Alfred Crowe.

Sir – By the passing of Alfred Crowe, Holt has lost another real native. He was born in the town and lived here for over 80 years. As a boy, Alfred Crowe might have been seen perched on the box of his father's carriage outside the railway station, waiting for visitors to alight from a train. Sometimes a traveller wanted to go to a distant village, and the only way to get there was by horse power. Alfred carried on his father's business and was always ready to give a free lift to anyone trudging along the road. He bought a Belsize motor-car. It went faster than the carriage, but was far less reliable, and he could not have the same affection for a contraption of tin plate as for the horse. However, Alfred Crowe continued his taxi business for all his working days. Between jobs, he tended his carrier pigeons in the yard; these served him faithfully and won him many cups. When the high street lamps were put up, Alfred's yard, the flint gable ends and rosy tiles showed sweet and homely against the dark. He passed his life in a pleasant place, and his widow and children live there, and of course his sister and helpmate, Rachel. – Yours faithfully, J.H. (Holt)

And the EDP editor adds: our contributor will readily be identified by the familiar initials.

A Holt Childhood – Dora Hills

There now follows the first in a regular series of short childhood memoirs, taken in the main from recorded conversations. It is a feature of material taken from this source that the topic follows the strength of a particular prompt of memory – and not any predictable sequence. For the convenience of the reader, I have organised these into broad categories.

Dora talks about family life

"My mother came from Bridgenorth in Shropshire; she met my dad in Holt when she came, at the age of eighteen or nineteen, to work with a lady whose husband worked at Gresham's. We moved from Peacock Lane to the house on Norwich Road when I was about six. I can particularly remember when Granny was dying; she lay in that front room where Yetman's now is, and they laid all straw all outside on the road so that she wouldn't hear the noise. Dad said to us, 'Would you go on the Hills and fetch her some of that nice spring water over?' So we brought the water back – she wanted some cool water. She died the day after. My dad carried us into the front room where we kissed her on the forehead which was icy cold.

Sometimes after school we would walk up to White House Farm for fresh milk. We would go into the cool dairy where the farmer's wife ladled out the milk into our jugs. We came back from the farm one day to find we had a new baby brother. On bath-night, we used to listen to *In Town Tonight* on the radio, that used to be lovely. The saucepans were boiling up on the old range, with the bath in front of the fire. The youngest went in first, then my mother would add some more water for the next one, and then some more when the other one come, and so on. She'd say, 'If you behave yourself, you can listen to Music Hall.' We'd sit all round that radio, in front of that fire, until it was time to go to bed. My dad would say, 'I'm going down to the fish and chip shop later, if you behave yourself you can have some.' And if we were asleep when he came home with them, he used to save them until the morning, and we had them for breakfast.

Gussy Holt used to light the lamps. A little man, and he used to ride his bicycle with his ladder on the side, and I can picture him now, when we lived on the Norwich road, he'd climb up his ladder and light his lamp, then off he'd go up the Norwich Road and do a few more. My dad used to say, 'Here comes Gussy!'

I remember my Uncle Reggie always wanted my younger sister Sylvia to go down to collect his Eastern Daily from Rounce and Wortley, where Starlings is now. She'd run down every day before school, for which he'd give her tuppence; it cost a penny halfpenny, and she was allowed to keep the change! We thought she was ever so lucky, she was better off than us!

Do you remember Bobby Owens, who lived up the Cley Road in one of those British legion houses? He came to the Church school with us. Well, one day he did something wrong, and was told he had to stay in and write so many lines. He didn't, he went home, and told his mother. She frog-marched him back down the street, back to the school – I could see all this, as we lived opposite the school – she made sure he did them!

pigeon loft

My dad kept pigeons, which he bred and raced. He sold some birds to a Mr Huntley, and the Christmas afterwards a large crate was delivered to our house; this contained one large Christmas cake and five small ones, each with our name on, which we kept until our birthday."

Neighbours

"There was a shop next to us, run by Mrs Boyce – she had everything in it. The thing is, she had a parrot, and this parrot would talk, and if you went in the shop, you wouldn't know if it was her talking to you or the parrot. I remember my dad sending me in there one day, for six pennyworth of cheese, and somebody said, 'Yes, can I help you?' and I answered, and of course it was the parrot! And she had a sister live with her, Miss Brundle, and she always used to play marching music. My friend's granny lived in one of those cottages over the road; she had a copper in the shed – she was a fat, jolly lady, often with a wool hat on and with her face red from the heat. Some evenings we would play cards with my friend's granddad in their little sitting-room, in front of the coal fire, while the old lady sat working at her sewing-machine. 'Lou' Bunkell, who lived in this tiny cottage up Norwich Road used to take in washing; now she had the copper in the same room she lived in, they only had that living-room, and a tiny kitchen. She used to take all the washing in from people up the Cromer Road in an old barrow. And she had to go across the road to the Carpenters to get her water. She'd wash and iron all this and she'd deliver it back up the Cromer Road, I can see her now pushing her barrow."

About Town

"I remember that day Queen Mary came to Holt. What I remember most about it is to do with my Uncle Dick, who worked on the roads. He was working the Stop and Go flags, and he stopped the car that Queen Mary was in! There were headlines in the local paper 'Holt Man Holds Queen Mary Up in her Limousine.' She was on her way from Kelling Hospital to Glandford Museum. I can picture her, we all stood in the town and she had this hat on. She was a tall, gracious lady."

The western side of Norwich Road

"Today, we see a green verge, trees and houses that are set back from the road. Formerly, there were the cottages shown in the photo on page 18 and then a residence with a wing whose gable gave on to the road. This was called Archdale House, a guesthouse for a while. As of now that wing is discernible only through a chimney-breast, left exposed at demolition, which is now on its outside wall. Next came a long building, immediately on to the road. This housed Tansley, a Sheringham-based photographer, and then Howard's dairy followed. This will feature in our next volume. After that came the Church School, whose entrance was directly on to the road, and then further small cottages."

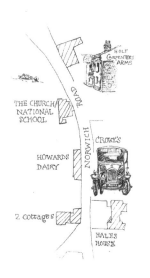

The Church School (or National School)

This school figures prominently in the memory of those who attended, but we cannot trace any records, nor can anyone supply a photograph. We know from Radford that the building was erected in 1842, opening to staff and pupils on January 6th 1843, after almost ten years of planning. Previously the children had been taught in the Shirehall. It was the initiative of local churchmen – the rectors of Holt and Letheringsett, and at its inception the trust deed placed the school in union with the National Society for the Promotion of the Education of the Poor

e 1911 Almanack lists the
ff as follows: Head Master,
Matthew Pearson, Assistant
stresses, Mrs Pearson, Miss
ace, Probationer, Miss Dann.

in the Principles of the Established Church – source of the both the alternative names by which it was known. Radford adds that 'In 1900 the school buildings were enlarged and improved at a cost of £500 by the munificence of the rector, the Rev. E. Brumell.'

Earle Kirby "I remember Helen Ramm as a kind and caring teacher who was specially interested in Dance. Her children's teams entered and won many festivals and competitions. I have to say that Miss Hewitt, however, had a fiercer reputation. Once when Canon Toft visited her lesson, he discovered her banging the heads of two boys together. On asking her which lesson it was, and hearing the reply, 'Scripture, Sir.' He said, 'Ah, very appropriate, Miss Hewitt, carry on.'"

Dora Hills remembers her for her acts of kindness – and other aspects, too.

Dora Hills "Miss Hewitt was very strict, but very kind. She used to bike up from Letheringsett to teach us. Children used to walk up to school from Letheringsett, and from further – Glandford. For these children she'd have a large kettle on the tortoise stove in the classroom, and at break time we Holt children would go home, but for she'd make a cup of cocoa for the others. What's more, if it was a very wet day when they were going back, she'd come across to my dad and hire a taxi for them. And I can see her at lunch-time, she'd take these children into the

nong the remembered
ildren are: the boys Pells and
rne [back row]; Evelyn
eeze, Audrey Camplin, the
l King, Annie Adcock and
llie White [centre row] and
orgina Bond, Emily Cook,
ura Green, Winnie Tyce, Lily
x and the Mears sisters [front
w].

shop and buy them shoes – out of her own money. But her hand was like a lump of beef coming across at you. She'd hit one ear – it's a wonder we're not all daft, really."

Mabel Gotts tells another story of Miss Hewitt.

Mabel Gotts "I hadn't been up that school long, I was in what they called Standard 3, my brother Ken was a bit of a lad, he didn't care whether he was Standard 3, Standard 5 or where he was, he was a good boy in his way. That morning – I hadn't been in that class long – she hummed a tune and we had to guess what it was. I realised what it was and shouted out, *Bluebells of Scotland*, I was right, but I didn't put my hand up. Well now, the book she had in her hand she threw at me, and that went past my ear by about an inch. My brother got out of his chair and said to her, 'If you throw a book at my sister again I'll throw a book at you!' Of course he had to go into Mr Pearson's then… but if that had hit me, that would have knocked me out, it was a big book. She had her good points, too, I'll admit that, but every so often she'd lose herself."

A triumphant departure!

"The day I left school, I went home in a Rolls Royce! A reverend and his wife wanted somebody to go and work at their place somewhere right in the country, and they sent me home with them to see my mother. My mother's response was: 'No, she's not going, she's not used to that.' But I sat in front with the driver!"

The boys at the Church school appeared to have matched their peers at the Senior School for inventive mischief – the school bell in its bell-cote on the roof had not worked for many years. Earle and three of his friends decided to be helpful by climbing to the roof and ringing the bell for Assembly. "We got stuck and got the cane," says Earle. He describes Canon Toft as a "lovely old man" – the school's patron, who took a hands-on interest in the school activities. He was Rural Dean and would come over from his home in Cley Old Rectory to visit the school every two weeks or so. He rather than Rev King, the chairman of managers, is remembered by Earle as being present in school.

Harold Cooke "There were two playgrounds, one for the girls, one for the boys, two large classrooms and a smaller classroom. I went there after two years at the Infants School. There were certain days the rector would come in for religious studies, Rev H A King,

Eva Lord Matt Pearson was a schoolmaster and his wife worked at the school, too, and they had a daughter called Maidie and a son called Clive. What he didn't know wasn't worth knowing. He was a good mixer, I should say. He nearly ran the town!

This photo is annotated on the reverse as follows:

Back row, from left to right: Miss Hawes, myself, Miss Bunkell, Miss Dame

Front row: Miss Chalker, Mr Pearson, Mrs Pearson

This is, then, a group photo of the combined staffs of both schools in Norwich Road at that time, the Infants School and the Church School. Post-1910.

NB Matt Pearson went on to become Town Clerk for many years.

sometimes he was helped by Rev Charles Tofts, whose arrival was always looked forward to. The first thing he did on coming in the room was to lay a heap of pennies on the desk at the front; if you answered the question right you got a penny, if you answered a question wrong he took one back; so you only hoped by the end of the exam you had some money left! It was quite a homely school; we had a dear old lady who used to clean the school, Mrs Effie Foster. On a Friday we used to go out for football or cricket to what is now the Country Park; by the time we'd walked up there, there wasn't much time to play! However, we did it every week on a Friday, whether it rained or whether it snowed, we had to march up there and march back."

nuary 11 1928. A goose elonging to Mr Fletcher took a ght over the town. nfortunately it collided olently with a chimney on Mr ant's house, bringing down e chimney pot and several icks and tiles. The goose elf fell dead at the feet of Mr Clarke, who was road-veeping.

The Northern End of Norwich Road

This delightful photo shows the point where Norwich Road runs into Obelisk Square. Notice that the photo bears the name Norwich Street. On the left is a run of small cottages, which come immediately after a doorway, which led into the Church School yard. Beyond these cottages stood a brick building, once a mortuary, then a Fire Station. On the right may be seen the Carpenters Arms, which was run for many years by the Gant family. According to near-neighbour Dora Hills, it was a very popular pub, and ideally placed for the

men who worked in the gasworks just down Letheringsett Hill. Cliff Watts' uncle was manager there, and Cliff remembers the role played by the Carpenters Arms in the daily routine of the stokers.

Cliff Watts "I tell you what, they used to spend a lot of time in there, those gas-boys did, after charging. That was hard work, that was, make 'em sweat, they had to put something back!"

There was – and still is – a yard of cottages to the side of the pub.

Obelisk Plain

The town pound was situated here. As we look from the end of the High Street, its precise location, according to a ground-plan in the Checkley collection, was in the left-hand front corner of the chapel grounds, half within the perimeter wall, half outside. Was it here that Holt gained the owl as motif?

> Some men of the town of Holt, the story goes, once caught an owl and put it in the pound for safe keeping. By next morning it had, of course, vanished.

Or here?

> An alternative story is that they put it the great waterspout of the church, hoping that it might drown in the next shower of rain. The bird, however, calmly flew up and soared away.

> *Folklores of East Anglia*

Whatever the exact origin of these tales, and despite their apparent significance, the people of Holt have ever since been called The Knowing Ones.

United Reform Chapel/United Methodist Church

The history of Methodism in Holt has already been written and published by Elizabeth Bellamy. It provides an enthralling read of a complex story. For the purposes of this volume, we need to know how Holt came to have three chapels, all part of Methodism, and all built within a period of thirty-four years – 1838–1872. The construction of this magnificent chapel was started in 1863 at the instigation of the Methodist Free Society, after a period of internal dispute within the Methodist movement. The issue at stake was that of lay leadership within the church, and in 1849, William Hardy Cozens-Hardy and others were expelled. There followed a London court case which centred on the financial background to the existing Wesleyan Chapel in New Street. As a result of this case – which they won – those expelled from Wesleyan

Methodism started a new Methodist Church in Holt, variously known as the Wesleyan Reformers, the Free Methodists and the United Methodists. The church on Obelisk Plain was designed by the noted Norwich architect Thomas Jeckyll, whose style featured a somewhat flamboyant use of red and cream bricks, designated informally as Streaky Bacon! In 1862, William H Cozens-Hardy, of Letheringsett, had given land on Obelisk Plain for a new church. By this time there was a large and thriving congregation. The structure is said to represent the early career of Thomas Jeckyll and to be one of the most significant examples of the taste for contrasted building materials which so delighted the mid-Victorians. It opened on Good Friday, April 3rd 1863.

The chapel has been the home of all Methodists in Holt since 1932, when the different strands of Methodism merged. Elizabeth Bellamy tells the complete story in her book.

THE RECTORY

BARCLAYS BANK

NEW STREET

to the Rectory

LETHERINGSETT HILL

GAS WORKS

HILL COTTAGES

MORGANS BREWERY

GALLOWAY

HORNE STONE MASON

THE KINGS HEAD

Craskes Chemist

blacksmith LOYNES YARD

HIGH STREET

LION HOUSE

MOULTONS OUTFITTERS

HILL HOUSE

THE LIMES
SCHOOL for GIRLS
late C19 early C20

HOLT CARPENTERS ARMS

THE UNITED METHODIST FREE CHURCH

NORWICH ROAD

Favourite watering hole of the gas boys

CHAPTER TWO

Chapter 2

This is the southerly aspect to the Rectory.

Rectory Life

In the last chapter we had mention of the Rectory on Letheringsett Hill. We heard, too, of 'Parson King', and the unwelcome arrival of a flood sweeping down from the Hills when Holt's children took pleasure from the building of dams – and even more, the taunting of their rector. Now, through a remarkable family memoir written in the 1980s, we may walk through that rectory gate and step inside the lives of the King family. The Rev Herbert King and his wife Lucy lived in the house between early 1909, when he took over the parish, and 1947, when he died. They had nine children, six of whom were born to them in Holt. Childhood in the house proved to have a lasting effect on all of the children, through the nature of the family relationships, of course, but also through the very special quality of the house and garden. Late in their lives they collaborated on the production of an eighty-page booklet in which they fondly recall their childhood years, including some vivid passages on aspects of life in Holt itself. We are incredibly fortunate to have been given access to this memoir, not only for the insights it offers, but also for the sheer joy it gives in reading. You will find extracts both in this chapter and throughout this volume, as they recall experiences associated with various parts of the town. But we start with the family home, as described by John King:

> Let me try and convey something of the quality of life at Holt rectory in the Teens and Twenties, for few families of our means and circumstances could have been more fortunately placed. The Rectory and its situation were gracious, the gardens extensive and varied, yielding some of the finest fruits

and vegetables (notably asparagus), even livestock, making it an idyllic home for young children to grow up and play in. We could fish for minnows, stickleback and red-throats in the pond, which had its resident moorhens and water-rats and a visiting king-fisher. And the stream was an endless source of delight. This ran from the pond and was itself supplied from Spout Hills, past the front lawn and side lawns, to disappear down a well which ran underground to the other side of the Letheringsett Road. We sailed boats and motor-boats and smaller craft down the stream. Mud-pies, dams and paddling gave endless pleasure. On the large front lawn, cricket was an early activity, later hockey and bicycle hockey. In the end father laid out a clock-golf putting green. In the very early twenties, with additional help, Cotts constructed a tennis court on a field let out to Ben Empson, the local hackney carriage hirer whom we patronised, and a great, often bitter rival of the Crowe family. The side lawn was a croquet lawn; and the drive up to the front door and the paths which led round the house were ideal places for bowling hoops, wooden and metal, and later for bicycling or motor-cycling around. Beyond the stream on the side lawns was rough unfilled orchard which led up to the woodland; and this whole area was a great place for war games, Red Indians, hide-and-seek – a fine place, too, if you wanted to 'get lost' for a spell!

It was a great place, too, for wild life. In the summer we heard night-jars, cuckoos and nightingales; chiff-chaffs and willow-warblers nested as well as white-throats, bullfinches and goldcrests, and a whole host of swallows and martins under the eaves or in the stable buildings. There were rabbits in the wood which we sometimes hunted with a borrowed dog; and the garden was well-provided with all sorts of trees and shrubs.

Owing to the vast size of the walled kitchen garden, potato orchard and the hill garden, it was essential for father to keep a gardener full time. Watson left us after the First World War to become a market gardener on his own; and no family can have been better served than we were by Herbert Cotts, who returning after the war after a bad gassing on the Western Front, devoted himself life and soul to the Rectory. He mowed the vast lawns, tended the innumerable flower-beds, dug and grew crops in all the orchards; kept hens, shared with father in rearing pigs, as Watson had done before him; but in addition he cleaned all the shoes daily, distempered rooms in the winter when he could not work out of doors, and was a happy, cheerful jack-of-all trades. He was a most trusted and loved member of the family, who worked for us for close on thirty years."

Beatrice Scarr (née King) has warm recollections, too.

The gardener Mr Cotts was more than a gardener. We adored him and he was a family friend. He came to us after the Great War, a very handsome young man with a moustache. He was married to his dear Fanny whom we always thought looked old enough to be his mother; but they were blissfully happy, although childless. I was always called Miss Beetrice and John was bor (boy) John. Miss was applied to all us girls, master to the boys. Fanny had a lot more than a double chin. She did not seem to have much neck, only one long big chin, or series of chins! She was famous for her home-made wines. Many a time in our adolescence when we visited the Cottses, we imbibed rather more than one glass and went tottering home: it is true 'home' was only about three hundred yards away. They lived in the little tied cottage belonging to the Rectory.

St. John's cottage

It was a large household, as these extracts indicate:

The year 1910, when I was born at Holt Rectory was a nice easy one from which to calculate my age. It was more memorable for the year George V came to the throne. I understand that a tea party in the garden was interrupted when my mother had to retire for my impending birth. Nurse Saye, who was summoned from London at each of the family births, was already there awaiting my advent... As I said, I was the fifth child in the family of nine. In spite of a moderate income, our parents were able to afford a cook, a nursery maid and a pantry maid or scullery maid. The latter made up the fires in the early morning and dealt with the oil lamps and other basic needs. My mother said it took an hour and a half for the maid to trim and fill the lamps each day. They were filled with paraffin in a special little room in the south wing of the house, reserved for general cleaning commodities. This is where the flowers were arranged, too.

Apart from Gardener Herbert Cotts, one other figure stands out – that of their cook, Maria.

Aunt Maria, the cook, was a dear, buxom woman with hair scraped back into a tiny bun. She was always 'Aunt Maria' to us as she was always visited by her niece, who, of course, would ask to see her Aunt Maria. My recollection of her is of a comfortable person in a blue and white pin-striped blouse, sleeves rolled up, strong arms plunging into a huge crock of bread-dough, kneading this huge dollop of dough 'sides to middle'. This was put into tins to rise further and baked in one of the ovens in the big kitchen range or sometimes in the small oven in the wall of the scullery, heated by a small fire in the wall below.

Aunt Maria, our cook, was a faithful friend for many a long year, until she retired to a small cottage at the top of Letheringsett Hill, where we used to visit her from time to time. (John King)

Jane Hales was much taken with Maria, whom she knew in later life, and in one of her newspaper articles traces her life story, the working part of which ended with the Kings. On the newspaper cutting from which this is taken, Pat Buxton, the youngest of the King children wrote 'Maria Meares, our cook/nanny/friend'. Most of Maria's life had been spent in service, including a spell in London where she fell ill, and in Norwich and the Fens. She then returned to her family, who by that time were living in a village in the Glaven valley. It is here we pick up her story.

Maria's last job as a cook was in a big rectory near her old home. There were nine children in that house, and she baked them great loaves for their teas. The rare baker's loaf – they gobbled that up like cake. Maria loved children and what she said to them was sometimes puzzling and often poetic. To the little boy running out of the gloom of her kitchen, she called: 'Don't you forget yer hat do a butterfly 'll light on yer head.' Maria's similes were not the conventional ones, but her own. When laid abed with a fever, she complained that the noises in her head were 'like the stones shiftin' on the shore.' She was keenly observant and could find her way for many miles about the countryside. When asked if she had ever been by road to King's Lynn, she replied, 'No, but I could git there seein' I know where it ter lay by readin' on the signposts.' She had a keen appreciation of life and delighted in the comforts of summer. Maria was a good eater, but disliked birds, rabbits and hares, doubtless because of a surfeit in early life. 'Them there ole tempests, I can't abide them', she would say. As for war, she looked upon it as a kind of periodic tempest, not on the whole as alarming as thunder and lightning. Bombs did not unduly disturb her, though she did sleep downstairs after a land mine had brought down an upstairs ceiling.

At the end of her life, Maria lived in 'a little totty house at the ind of a yard.' In the summer days she locked her door and off she went to the garden of her late mistress, to wander amongst the flowers and vegetables, picking up apples and talking to herself, 'If no-one wasn't nigh nor by.' She was always contented, except when she lost her key, 'That there

37

Family portrait on the occasion of the parents' Silver Wedding.

From left to right. The boys in the back row, John, Francis, Philip.

Seated on chairs, Katherine, Mary, father, mother, Margaret, Beatrice

Seated on the rug, Patricia and Dorothea

mucky ole key, that ain't nowhere!", she would complain in great agitation.

John King There is no doubt we were happy as a family; we got on well with each other, and if temporarily two were at variance, well there were so many of us you could shift your company for the time being. So many, indeed, that we used to be amused at father who sometimes would name two or three of his children before he hit on the right name. Our dining-room was spacious enough to hold a magnificent mahogany table which had at least three leaves to it and which could seat as many as twenty on occasions. Until the thirties, we were generally all present in holiday time. Family meals always started with a grace, just as the day started with family prayers. For the latter, we assembled, domestics as well, in the drawing-room and were each issued with a thin red paper-backed prayer book. The only escape from this, as we grew older and less willing to attend, was to be 'taken short' at the crucial moment, but in our house, only two could play this game!

Christmas was a great occasion in the days of our youth. Bodies of carol singers collected with lanterns to sing as far away as Kelling sanatorium, and at Home Place, a crammer's

t Buxton, the youngest of
e nine children, entitled
r contribution to the
nily memoir *Recollections
 an Afterthought*:

ras very lonely and starved
 playmates. The older
embers of the family had
t home in term time for
eir various colleges,
hools and jobs, leaving
ea (who went to Christ's
ospital when I was about
e) and Philip who was at
esham's. He was not
rticularly scintillated by
y company, and was no
ubt occupied with
isbehaving elsewhere. The
rents seemed very old
ey were 52 and 42 when I
as born), they were good
d kind, but did not play
th me much. Pa didn't
em to remember my name
o well...

establishment... In anticipation of untold wealth in our stockings, we sent for Gamages' catalogue and scanned its pages to decide what we should buy. Our ardour was never damped by the fact that each year came and passed without the wealth being showered upon us. But we did get generous money presents from the Welsfords. Grandpa and Grandma King came each year from London, and after Christmas dinner, Grandpa stood on the drawing-room carpet, called us hither and announced that he was going to give us a 'portrait of the Queen'. We all expected a literal portrait, but we were not dismayed when he gave us each a sixpence. Perhaps it was his Victorian upbringing which made him insist on 'the Queen', for she had been dead a dozen years. Edward V11, too, had gone, and we were well into George V's reign. Judging by the number of bun-pennies which were available for years and years, it is quite possible he collected sufficient 'Queen Victoria' sixpences for his grandchildren. Another great delight of that time was the arrival of a hamper from Sandringham. Queen Mary sent each year to the clergy in Norfolk who had large families, a splendid hamper filled with good things to eat: figs, nuts, dates, fondants, a Christmas pudding, tangerines and the like. There may even have been a bottle of port. The turkey came from Sir Alfred Jodrell, a warm admirer of father, who used to drive up to Holt Church on Sundays in state, with his landau with its crest on the doors and a liveried driver. On one occasion he sent a swan.

We grew up in a musical atmosphere. One of my very early recollections, and one that made the deepest impression on me, was mother playing and singing *Rock of Ages Cleft for Me*, which had been sung at her mother's funeral. And the memory of it still made her very sad. She certainly conveyed to me as a child the sense of loss and loneliness, the awful gap her mother's death had made in her life. Our Aunt Maud was more than a passable pianist, and she played Beethoven sonatas, Mendlesohn's Songs Without Words and a whole host of other works.

The eldest son, Francis, thinks back to the range of vehicles that were commonly in use:

It was a world where the motor-car was a comparative rarity. I can remember clearly the day when I saw (noticed) a motor-car for the first time as it went down the hill towards Letheringsett. People went about on bicycles, or on foot much more, or in carriages, cabs, dog-carts, pony-traps or in brakes. The well-to-do had carriages with coachmen or grooms in attendance. Farmers used dog-carts which were high, springy

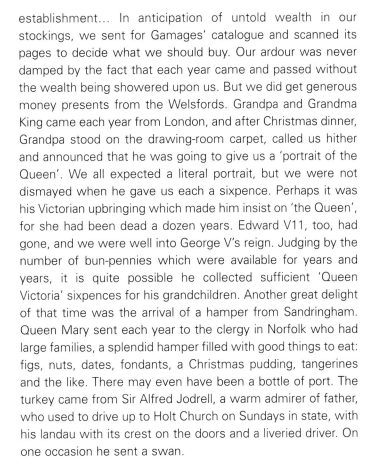

Looking down Letheringsett Hill... Turn left just before the cottages and you come to the gasworks.

and rather elegant. The pony-traps were often driven by women. I have been many a ride to the surrounding villages in a pony-trap – great fun when the skittish animal got excited and bolted, its hooves hammering on the underneath side of the floorboards. Wagonettes or brakes were used for outings, choir outings, cricket matches, expeditions and school treats. There is a photograph of father, reins in hand, about to set off with the family, as it was then, in an obviously hired vehicle. I have been with a Holt cricket team to play a match on the other side of Cromer at Lord Suffield's in some such vehicle as a wagonette and on other outings of the same sort. These things do not exist now except as 'period pieces' or in museums, or at horse shows. Indeed, carriages were so much the only means of transport that Holt had the rival cab firms, Empson and Crowe, both men powerful, thickset and fierce. Father once had to intervene in a free fight between these two, outside Holt station, over a potential customer just off the train. I think he survived without injury.

I can remember a visit from one rather grand lady, a real live Admiral's wife at that! She swept up the drive in her elegant carriage (she had been invited to tea) and was not at all pleased to find that the parents had entirely forgotten about this. We children stood open-mouthed on the lawn as the drama unfolded.

Children's parties involved going in cabs, which was rather fun, especially at night. We were wrapped in rugs and enjoyed the mysterious glimpses of the lanes by carriage lamplight. The cabs smelt of hay, stables, horse manure, all of which helped to give atmosphere to an exciting experience. One regular invitation was a hay-party in Stody, but that was a day affair at haymaking time. The hay was already cut and standing in mounds into which we joyfully flung ourselves, and round which we played hide-and-seek.

Here, Francis gives this evocative portrait of the town:

We did not feel too cut off, however, as from the upper windows, Holt could be seen laid out on its hilltop, a little in the manner of a mediaeval town. A better view of this sort could be seen from the glebeland just above the wood – a varied skyline comprising amongst other buildings a windmill, a chapel, a stately and handsome tall brick water-tower, a chapel with a spire, and in front of this, the local gasworks, and a nearby folly, a boxy little house which had had battlements added to give it an air of importance. From the glebe one could survey the Holt panorama with sound effects thrown in. From the distance

came cocks crowing in the backyards, the sound of the smith's hammer and anvil, sharp and clear, distant noises from the railway station – trains clanking in sidings, whistles from the engines and the rumble of carriages on the single line to Melton Constable; horses clip-clopping, dogs barking, cars in Holt changing gear with horns hooting, Holt citizens passing the time of day with each other – all this gave a wonderful impression of a community in full swing, somewhat on the lines of Under Milk Wood. Down below on the Spout Hills was the pumping-station, a handsome little brick building in the same style as the water-tower. This emitted a very comforting noise – chump chump chump-chump chump chump – comfortable to the body also, as by standing over the grating just outside its walls one could bask in the glorious warmth of the exhaust gas which shot up trouser legs and ballooned out the skirts of the girls.

The Gasworks

Between the Holt Rectory and the town lies the main access to Spout Hills. This is the site, too, of the former gasworks, and the group of cottages, set in a yard, known as Hill Cottages. John Jarvis now describes the works.

John Jarvis "When you went in to the gasworks, the first thing you saw was a long bank of furnaces – retorts we called them; there must have been at least eight, but not all of them were in use at any one time. They had cast-iron oval doors, with a steel front – similar to oven doors; once these had been dragged open, the gas-men used to shovel in the small nuts of coal, like the coals a blacksmith used. We used to stand and watch them. First, they'd fetch a barrow, then go over to the huge heap of coal piled up in the yard; they'd fill up the barrow, take it back inside and empty it. What always amazed me was their tremendous skill in throwing these nuts right to the back of the retorts. Now these were about twelve feet long, twenty inches wide, ten high. Those men had it down to a fine art, there wasn't one bit of coal that hit those sides. They'd close the door and seal it with a putty type of stuff. It would then burn for several hours. Afterwards, they would open it up – and that would be all coke inside. Every time they opened it after a burning, they lit a taper, which they put near the door, and there'd be a small explosion caused by the residue of gas inside. They'd pull the coke out with a retort hoe, down on to the steel floor, where it would be hosed down. Then they would take it outside to be collected by customers, who'd take it away in hessian sacks. The tar was extracted too, and that would be piped to the tanks that stood outside. Tar, gas, coke – all out of the coal. Each retort would burn for a three or four hours, and there'd be about six going at once, day and night. To

...ff Watts "My uncle used ...go round emptying the ...s meters – he had a big ...ather bag, and by the time ... got round, that was heavy ...hey were those old ...nnies in there. Poor old ...b, if ever there was a ...ddy there, he'd say, 'What, ... you want a penny?' He'd ...ve 'em one. He was as ...od as gold."

keep those heaps of coal piled high, there was a continuous stream of horses and carts coming from the station, through the town, up to the gasworks – that just went on through the day.

Now the gas-holder. It was circular, with an exterior metal framework, as you'd expect. Seen from the inside, the circumference was built up with a brick parapet, which acted as a retaining wall for the pool of water at the base. This was to purify the gas as it bubbled through into the holder, a structure with a metal dome. Evidently, this rose and fell according to the demand from the town and the work-rate of the gasmen, who would take a peep at its height every so often. In this way they knew when they would have to start shovelling again."

Edith Pointin "Marjorie Garrett, whose father ran the gas-works, was my school-friend and we would love to watch the men fill the huge retorts with coal and then later taking it out as coke. Sometimes a kind of tar would stick round and we would knock it off and it made grand shapes of animals."

Hill Cottages

A Holt Childhood – Mabel Gotts

Dr Hales knew of the healthy environment offered by the gasworks, and persuaded Mr and Mrs Peck to move to Hill Cottages when the opportunity arose. Their daughter, Mabel Gotts, now talks of her childhood.

Mabel Gotts "We moved there, because when I was born, I took the shock instead of my mother; I was so small, you could have got me in a milk jug! Anyway, I was rather a job to bring up and old Dr Hales told my mother, 'If you can get her anywhere near the gasworks, that will do her the world of good.' In due course there was this house going down near the Hills, which Mother applied for and got. And from then on, he was right, I got on like a house on fire. People used to come, and say Coo! That horrible old smell of that old gas, I used to love it!

I was born 1916, and the night I was born the Zeppelins came over. My eldest brother Val wanted to know where I had come from, and old Dr Hales told him the Zeppelins had dropped me! And when I was a little bit older, and my mum asked him to hold me, he said, 'If it hadn't been for the Zeppelins we wouldn't have had her!' That Doctor Hales used to shout at you, I used to be terrified of him!"

Mabel developed unusual tastes.

"Mother used to notice that mould was going out of her pots and her flowers, and the wood, where it was rotten, used to be taken off the gateway – and it was me, I used to eat it! We had a little coal-house, and I used to sit there and eat coal and coke. That's not all, I used to get a spoon and take the red out of bricks; Mother got worried and called old Dr Hales. 'You let her alone' – I can see her now telling me – 'You let her alone,' he said, 'that's doing her more good than what we can, that's giving her a lining to her stomach!' I can see myself now, sitting in that coal-house."

There was plenty going on to interest the children.

"On market day they used to drive in the cattle and sheep down there, because there was a weighing machine. There were tubs of tar laying about, too, we used to play on them! There were four cottages in the yard; the Moores were in the end house, then there was an old couple, Mr and Mrs Baldry, then Mrs Webster, then us, we were in the other end. Robert Moore worked on the railway; now as a child, I used to think he was a clever man, and I'll tell you why. You remember those old-fashioned armchairs, with wings? He would be laying back in there, with his dinner on his stomach, and his feet on the mantelpiece. I said to my dad one day, 'Why don't you do what Mr Moore do?' 'I should get wrong off your mother, if I did that!' It has to be said, Mrs Moore and Mrs Webster didn't get on – there was only one toilet, and they had to take it in turns to keep it clean. That's until Mrs Webster had one done for herself in her shed. Now my mother put in for one of the houses built down the Peacock Lane, and we were well away to have one. But meanwhile, Mrs Webster, unbeknown to my mother, approached the Council and arranged for the Moores to have it, not us. So they moved away, not us. We stopped there."

Mabel's Saturday job

"Mrs Webster did a huge amount of washing for the Gresham's School – not only that, the surplices for the church, too. She had that little old pram, and on a Saturday she used to get me to deliver it all. It didn't matter if it was hailing, raining, snowing, whatever it was doing, I had to go, and I got tuppence. There were five lots I had to deliver, they were sitting all on top of each other – there was a big basket first, then a smaller basket, then a bundle and another bundle, I hadn't left school at this time. I often used to be perished when I got back. Then I had to polish all the furniture. After that, Mrs Webster had more

errands for me. I had to go to Mrs Buck, who was her sister, who had that shop on the corner, and she got me to take things up to the baker's for her to be baked – 'cos people used to take their joints up there then. We used to think tuppence was the world, in those days."

A frightening experience

"One Saturday night in winter we'd been up to Boyce's in the Norwich Road; I'd been with my mother and she thought she'd got everything. But when we got home, she said, 'Oh, I've forgotten the birdseed. Will you go after it or shall I go?' and I didn't want to go after it and I didn't want to be left alone, anyway I said I'd go. I got up to the shop, got the birdseed and got back as far as Skrimshire's house, and when I got there, a man came out of the gateway and tried to get hold of me. It was dark, you couldn't see much. I remember shrieking, they heard me right up against Briggs, the jewellers, so you know the noise I made! I don't remember running down the Hill, but I did, I collapsed indoors, and of course I couldn't tell what had happened to me."

Mabel talks of her parents and family background

"My mother (May Emilia White) was born in Great Snoring and at the age of sixteen came to Holt into service, went down Valley Lane where she worked for the Shaws. Mr Shaw was Music Master up at Gresham's school. My mother was nursemaid to their son Sebastian, who became an actor. But she didn't like Holt, all the years she lived here, she didn't like it, and I never did know why; whether it was because she was brought up right in the country, I don't know. Of course I used to go and stay with my grandparents a lot in the summer holidays, spent most of my summer holidays over at Great Snoring, used to take the forces (?) to my grand-dad in the fields, that kind of thing. My mother was one of the founder members of the Methodist

WESLEYAN
CHAPEL
1838

Sisterhood. I used to do a lot of singing at the Methodist Chapel, then I taught for several years at the Sunday School... My father (Thomas Augustus Peck) was originally from East Harling, but when he was quite small his family moved to Great Walsingham, and he worked for Lees of Holt all his working life, from the age of sixteen, I believe. He used to go out with the horse and cart – and he came home from that so tired, I used to do his books for him, to get them done, when I was old enough."

Sundry recollections of her childhood years

"I always remember my brother giving me tuppence to go and buy him some cigarettes, some Woodbines. And the shopkeeper let me have them! He took them on the Hills, he managed to get some matches, 'I'm going to have a little smoke, I shall be all right, but you mustn't tell Mother, you mustn't tell Dad.' I stopped there while he did it, and, well, he went green, he went green as the bushes! I had to go home and tell Mother that he wasn't well on the Hills – so they found out then!

There was a Mr Oddy who lived up the Norwich Road, they were a well-known family, the Oddys, anyway he had a terrier dog, a ginger colour, and my father had one the same, the only two in Holt. One day Mr Oddy came down to see my dad and he said, 'I've lost my dog, will you sell me yours?' And my dad said, 'No, I'm afraid not.' He said, 'Well, I'll give you fifty pound.' Well that was a lot of money years ago. 'No, we've had that dog since my little girl was three years old.'"

Obelisk Plain

Archie Checkley The pineapple-topped obelisk at Holt is one of a pair of gateposts from Melton Park, the other being given to Dereham in 1757. On each of the four sides the distances to various places are cut into the stone and cause great interest. During World War Two, in order to avoid helping the enemy, Dereham dumped theirs down a deep well (it was still there in 1987). Holt, being the clever old owls that they are, just whitewashed theirs.

From the 20s onwards, Percy Dyson had his garage down the lane behind Mrs Buck's sweet shop on the corner.

Hill House and The Skrimshires

...e view up High Street from
...l House, home of the
...rimshire family.

...the yard to the left of Walter
...rne's workshop was the
...cksmith's forge of the
...ynes family. Above, four
...nerations of the Loynes
...nily, not in a direct line, but
...with the Christian name of
...bert: Robert Loynes,
...28–1911, great-great-uncle of
...bert John Loynes,
...46–1911, grandfather of
...bert Edmunds Loynes, uncle
...Robert Repps Loynes, born
...1906.

Dr John Truscott Skrimshire inherited the medical practice based at Hill House from his father, as had Dr Hales. In that era, a medical practice was, in effect, the family business, often passed down through several generations. He bought Hill House from the Cozens-Hardy family in 1881, and it has remained in (extended) family ownership ever since. There were four children born to Dr JT Skrimshire and his wife Lizzie, two boys, Jack and Harry, and two girls, Dorothy and Amy. Both Jack and Harry went on to train as doctors, returning early in their careers to Norfolk. Jack acquired a practice in Melton Constable, while Harry subsequently took over his father's Holt practice in Hill House. (When Holt people now talk of Dr Skrimshire, it is Harry to whom they refer.) Now the daughters! In due course, Dorothy came to marry, and yes, she married a doctor, Joseph Gillam, who also set up practice in Holt in the early years of the twentieth century – but at the other end of town! It was Dr Gillam who had the house called Shrublands (now The Beeches) built in Hempstead Road on the occasion of his marriage in St Andrew's, Holt, to Dorothy Skrimshire on Thursday, July 25th 1901. They lived there for several years, and had four children. But more of the Gillams when we reach the eastern end of town – back now to Hill House. Dr Harry Skrimshire practised from here for much of the first half of the century. Neither he nor his other sister Amy, who was blind, married, both living in the house. (We shall return to the work of Dr Harry Skrimshire in the next volume.)

Walter Horne worked here as a stonemason, with the blank slabs awaiting his chisel propped against the wall. The south-facing façade to his shop supported a vine. His son Reggie died in the First World War, and the business was taken over by a firm called Palmer & Gardner, Monumental Sculptors. The whole building is now Barnham and Kings.

The original purpose of the chapel-like building (now Nicholsons) remains unknown.

One of the daughters weds.

Jane Hales:

> Opposite, across the Plain, is the high house now called the Roundways, formerly the Corner House, or the Lower House. Here lived John Clarke (1786–186?). He was a wine merchant, an auctioneer and an estate agent, and at one time had managed a property in the West Indies. He was also a great man in the Vestry (forerunner of the Parish Council) and Visitor of the Workhouse, and was concerned in the planting of trees in the Cromer Road. John Clarke was bad-tempered at times, for he had the gout, due perhaps to too much port wine.

At The Limes, left, there was a school run by Mrs Reid, who is pictured standing at the gate. Very little information has been forthcoming about her establishment. We do know that she had daughters, who set a few hearts fluttering. Henry Hobart, for one, recalls caddying, as a boy, for a Reid daughter out golfing on the Hills. Mrs Reid was prominent in town affairs, sitting on the Parish Council for a number of years.

High Street

HB Moulton is listed in Kelly's 1896 as clothier and boot-dealer. But by the time of the 1901 census he must recently have died, as the listing reads 'Moulton, Minnie, Head of Family, Widow, 33, Clothier'. The couple had six children, the youngest a baby of eleven months at the time of the census. Their eldest son Herbert W Moulton, born 1892, took over the business as a young man. We have this photo (opposite), dated September 1910, showing him and other employees standing in front of the shop. Responsibility must have come to him easily, as he is listed in prominent roles in the town from the twenties onwards. He became, among other things, Chairman of the Parish Council and chairman of the British Legion, a major organisation in the town in the twenties and thirties.

David Durst, industrial archaeologist, has made a particular study of this building. He did so in connection with research

he undertook in the 1990s at the instigation of NNDC Planning Department, following an application from the owners of Lion House (now Betty's) to demolish a small, lean-to building on the side of their property. He had come to identify this as a smokehouse. In the course of his researches, he discovered that there had probably been both a

ung Bert Moulton with his ff at Lion House.

coach-builder and grocer based in the two properties in the second half of the nineteenth-century – both buildings carry date-stones, with the initials JA inscribed in each. We know that J Ainger was a coach-builder.

There remains, however, something of a mystery here, as this building has all the hallmarks of a nineteenth century chapel, but we can nowhere find any positive identification. It is not, for example, mentioned in *Methodism in Holt*, Elizabeth Bellamy's lucid guide to a complicated history. There was no other nonconformist sect settled in the town for any length of time, if a scrutiny of nineteenth-century directories is a reliable guide, apart from the Quakers, whose meeting-house was on land adjacent to the present Post Office. See Chapter 8.

An exhaustive study led David Durst to this conclusion: 'The best fit to all facts would arise if the Wesleyan Reformers had built the chapel in around 1850 (stylistically probable), then moved to larger premises in 1862/3 (their chapel on Obelisk Plain) and sold their old place to Mr Ainger the coach-builder. He rebuilt or remodelled his house in 1863, and in 1865 adapted the chapel. Perhaps his family ran a grocery from the chapel and lived next door.'

Galloway, now Richard Scott Antiques, was generally approved by Holt children. The building on the left with the -OB just visible, was an ironmonger's called JACOB. Its proprietor was not a popular figure.

Mabel Gotts "We used to call him Tin Ribs Jacob – his sho was all dark – all sorts of funny things about him, after anybod had been in, he'd go round and check that everything was st there. He was enough to frighten you, he'd come up fror behind somewhere when you went in. He had a Mrs Burto who used to be his housekeeper, she was rather a refine woman, as a matter of fact, she was very nice – how ever sh got there I'll never know, but some of the other women wh used to go there weren't very nice. That was a ghostly place the bell would clang."

Morgan's Brewery below.

Looking up the High Street on a warm summer day, awnings out on Moulton's, parasol on the pram. Our friend with the panama is one step ahead of the photographer! Note the pre-tarmac road surface, t quality of the pavements, the cobbled gutters. And here's a 1915 lett of complaint in *The Post*:

'Holt people are still wondering where the Holt watering-cart is. Summer is nearly here and yet the streets have not been watered th season. People who pay rates deserve to receive some consideration

ane Hales has rather a dismal recollection of Jacob too, nd in the telling, confesses to an unlikely passion.

Nobody was ever seen to enter that shop, but the writer, who in those days had an insatiable desire for nails, used to push open the door, which had a bell, and from the murky depths would emerge an old man.

Craske, Chemist

Thomas Augustus Craske (born 1854) came from a long line of chemists in the town. He was at the same time bank agent to Gurney's Bank, then farmer at Weybourne. Bernard Craske (born 1881), his great-nephew, took over the business shortly after the First World War, and ran it until he sold up to Paterson's in the fifties.

Another view of Moulton's, below, with a window, left, full of boaters.

ore the rain of Tuesday afternoon, dust was flying about in all ctions, constituting a real nuisance. According to a member of the t Parish Council, the parish watering-cart is undergoing its 'spring n'. Surely this ought to have been done weeks ago, so as to be ly for work early in the spring. It is time 'new blood' was oduced on the Parish Council – men who will see that the essary work is carried out at the proper time. Holt is something e than a country village and there should be a proper system of et watering. – a Pedestrian'

Morgans was a Norwich-based brewery which went through a period of expansion at the turn of the century. Not only had they bought out Edward Carter Cooper (listed in these premises in the 1890 edition of White's) but they had also acquired the Letheringsett Brewery in 1895.

Edith Pointin "Morgans Brewery made beer in the premises through from New Street to High Street. Men went out each day with horses and drays to deliver beer to all the villages around."

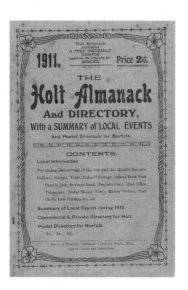

Street Talk

There now follows the first selection from the diary pages of one of the Holt Almanacks, that for 1911. The Almanack was a small booklet produced annually by the town's printers, Rounce and Wortley. Published on low-cost paper, and priced at twopence, it was clearly designed to be available to everybody. It listed all the key personalities, with their roles in the church, Parish Council, football or bowls club etc. It featured a diary of important events in the town for the last twelve months. It also provided health tips for the family, ran advertisements for various commercial services in the town – builders, for example – and gave a list of residents' addresses. For the purposes of our researches, these details are absolutely invaluable – and yet only four issues (for the years largely covered by this volume, 1900–1929) have been traced. These document the years 1911, 1916, 1925 and 1929. The diary pages are a real joy. They record events in a way which gives an intriguing picture of life in the town. They report particularly on a full range of social events – sporting fixtures, drama productions, club meetings and so on. In addition, they record the deaths of notable personalities and the completion, for example, of a new building.

But there is another major dimension, too, to these entries. The information given is one thing, but through the facts we learn, incidentally, so much more of the way of thinking prevalent at the time. The use of language is subtly different from ours today, and this very difference serves to reveal the framework of thought and the attitudes current in those years.

9 November 1909. The death occurred of Mr William Leggatt. The deceased gentleman, who was in his seventy-sixth year, had been in a precarious state of health for some considerable time and his decease therefore was not unexpected. By his death Holt has lost one of its most prominent inhabitants. There was hardly a public office in Holt and District that the late gentleman had not occupied, and occupied with credit and distinction to himself and with profit to the district. First and foremost, however, he was a Holt man and he took a leading part in anything which pertained to the good of the town.

12 November 1909. In the presence of a large and representative gathering, the mortal remains of the late Mr William Leggatt were interred in the family burial place in the family churchyard. The deceased gentleman had for so long filled a high and honourable place in the life of Holt that a large number of the inhabitants of the town and district desired, by their presence at the funeral, to show their regard for the family and pay the deceased gentleman a last token of respect.

27 January 1910. The Annual Meeting of the Workmen's Club was held, and the Hon Secs (Messrs H Vince and CW Jex) were able to present an excellent report and balance sheet. A profit of £7 1s 1d was made on the year's working, thus increasing the balance in hand to £13 2s 4d. An honorarium was voted to the Hon Secretaries and a motion expressive of the Club's thanks for their past services was adopted with acclamation.

24 January 1910. This day was the eve of the polling in connection with the North Norfolk election, and both parties held meetings, the Conservatives in the Oddfellows Hall, and the Liberals in the Concert Hall.

25 January 1910. Animated scenes were witnessed, when the youth of the town demonstrated loudly and enthusiastically. On the 26th the declaration of the poll took place at Aylsham, the figures being:

Mr Noel Buxton	5,189
Mr H Douglas King	4,604
Liberal Majority	585

1 February 1910. A meeting of the Parish Council was held. It was agreed to re-form the Burials Committee and proceed with the task of providing a burial ground with as little delay as possible.

17 February 1910. The Draughts match between the Letheringsett Reading Room and the Holt Workmen's Club took place at Letheringsett. Holt won by 22 games to 14.

1 March 1910. At the special meeting of the Parish Council, the amended scheme of the Board of Education relative to the Gresham's School local scholarships was considered, and the proposals of the Board were generally approved.

4 March 1910. Lord Hastings was elected without opposition as County Councillor for the Holt Division.

31 March 1910. The comic opera *The Duchess of Bosnia* was given under the management of Dr and Mrs de Beauvais, whose success in the production of *The Giant's Bride* in 1909 will not be readily forgotten. *The Duchess of Bosnia* was an opera full of bright dialogue and pretty and effective situations; the musical numbers were melodious and catching and were well rendered. Everything necessary for the production had been well prepared and the performance was a great success, the large audience testifying to their pleasure in no unstinted manner.

25 April 1910. There was a big entry in all departments at Holt Fair. A large number of buyers were present in addition to a representative gathering of local farmers and dealers.

30 April 1910. The end of the football season, which was most successful, Holt United easily winning the Rippingall Shield with an unbeaten League record. In all matches, they won 20 and drew 3, losing only 3. Goals scored were: 97 for, 26 against. W. Horne, with an aggregate of 43 goals, was the chief goal-scorer for the club.

6 May 1910. The death of King Edward VII. There is but one topic of conversation in the street, one thought in every mind, our gracious King Edward VII is dead. Over his coffin the air has rung with eloquent eulogies and touching tributes of regret and no-one has protested that more was said than the sorrow of the day required. King Edward ruled in our hearts as well as over our land, and we shall miss him sorely; miss that engaging smile, that quick perception of the right thing at the right moment, that keen and kindly sympathy for all, high or low, that intense desire for honourable peace and fellowship at home and abroad. We sorrow for his decease, we sympathise with the noble lady who won all our hearts when she came, a winsome bride – 'Sea-king's daughter from over the sea' – and has held them in her keeping ever since.

23 May 1910. Opening of the new Infants School, which is an especially fine erection, and Messrs CT Baker are to be commended for the excellence of their work.

6 June 1910. The monthly competition on the Lion Green for the 'Douglas King' Cup took place, Mr AR Jacob beating Mr AH Page in the final, by 11 points to 7.

9 June 1910. The 'Rippingall Trophy' was played for on the Feathers Green. In the final, Mr H Bond, after leading 9 – 3, had to acknowledge defeat

to Mr L Hughes, who played a fine uphill game, and finally won by 11 points to 10.

11 June 1910. The members of Cley and Holt Workmen's Club met in friendly rivalry at Cley, and the homesters won by 83 points to 37.

21 June 1910. Mr W Tipple defeated Mr M Pearson by 9 points to 4 in the first competition for the 'Douglas King' Cup on the Victoria Green.

28 September 1910. The death occurred of Mr E Dawson Rogers, the founder of the Eastern Daily Press, and a prominent figure in journalism. Mr Rogers, who had reached the venerable age of 87, was born in Holt and was educated at the Gresham's school.

5 October 1910. Mr PM Crosthwaite held an enquiry into the application of the Parish Council to borrow £500 for the provision of a burial ground. He visited the proposed site and expressed his entire approval therewith.

7 October 1910. At the Gresham's School there was a very fine lecture on Charles Kingsley, given by Mr AC Benson, MBO. The lecturer's personal acquaintance with Kingsley enabled him to paint some very graphic pictures, enlivened by some really humorous anecdotes.

Lillian May Shipp (born 1907), riding high and sitting pretty.

Both buildings on the right have gone. In their place we have Starlings and the present Barclays Bank.

Barclays Bank

This solid edifice, of magnificent brickwork, was built in the 1890s and demolished in the late 1950s. At the time of its construction, it must have seemed a metropolitan intruder, built with a type of brick only available in North Norfolk since the completion of the railway in 1884. The information below was provided by Tony Ringer, whose father worked there.

Tony Ringer "The entrance was in the near corner, with double doors leading into the bank chamber; there was a massive mahogany counter running left to right (parallel with New Street). There were two additional counters behind the main one, where men sat at high stools to work. On the far wall was a doorway leading down a concrete stairway to the bank vaults. The Manager's office was to the right of the doorway.

The bank premises themselves, though imposing, were nothing compared to the residence of the manager. This took up the rest of the building. On the very corner where New Street meets High Street was the dining-room, access to which came through a hall with a front door onto New Street, and an internal door from the bank. Beyond the hall was the main staircase, and then the breakfast room and kitchen. Access to a second staircase was from here; also, a back door led onto a courtyard. Upstairs was a square landing, off which led two bedrooms, and a massive lounge which could accommodate thirty people with ease; the bay window looked over the High Street. The top floor had one huge room and two or three others. From various windows there were panoramic views – to the sea over Cley/Salthouse, down the High Street to Old School House and Church Lane, across to the water tower. Not forgetting the garden, which lay to the rear of its neighbour on New Street – the Literary Institute."

The Preston family

One of the considerable pleasures of undertaking the researches for this book has been the discovery of the Preston photos. The phenomenon is of course well known to collectors and other initiates, but for us it was a gradual process of revelation. Quite simply we slowly became aware of a large number of very good photos of all kinds on subjects to do with Holt and its environs. Some had the name 'Preston' printed on the front, while others didn't. Some had a tell-tale flourish when a name was handwritten, others hadn't. All of them evince a freshness of treatment, a fine sense of composition, and a fond familiarity with the subject. They are very sharp in detail and have a high quality finish. Many adorn the pages of this book.

We do not yet know a great deal about the family, but for our purposes, we may start with William Preston, who in Kelly's directory of 1875 is listed as 'teacher of music, printer, bookseller and stationer, and fancy repository and farmer'. There was also Arthur Preston, a machine printer, who

Next to the bank stood the elegant premises of Arthur Preston, The Reliance Printing Works. His workforce are keen to feature in the photo taken by the itinerant photographer employed by the publisher of this postcard, Bell! A few years after this view was taken, Arthur Preston sold the business to Rounce and Wortley, probably around 1908. His sons opened a shop on Market Place now housing Florabunda.

published work of all descriptions. This included the Holt Almanack, complete with its diary, auctioneers' posters and catalogues, bags, price-lists, club books, mourning cards etc. Arthur's three sons, Thomas, Sidney and Chamberlain were part of their father's workforce at The Reliance Printing Works, High St, Holt (c1904). It is these three sons who developed the photography business in the town. They would go out on photographic missions on a trade bike, with the tripod strapped to the crossbar and the wooden box-camera lying in the tray in front. They worked both on a commission basis and they developed a style we might today call photo-journalism – except, of course, that the practice of including photos in newspapers was yet to emerge. A particularly striking set of images was taken on August 26th 1912 during the floods, when there was great devastation in Norfolk following a prolonged downpour. The brothers were out and about in Holt the next day, taking photos of rivers in spate, flooded fields, deep craters in roads, broken bridges and upturned carts. The resulting pictures are remarkable.

We know also of an Eva Preston and a Mary Preston, who we assume to be sisters to these photographers.

We end this chapter with such information as we have on the remaining properties on High Street, and with two photos taken by the Preston brothers. The first shows the shopfront of their neighbour, Lee. The left-hand window offers alcohol and the right-hand one is festooned with a range of tobacco products – Capstan Navy Cut, Wills, both well-known brands in the golden age of smoking. If the interior were better lit, we could identify more of the same inside, no doubt!

The Kings Head was run by the Outlaw sisters and an ostler.

Edith Pointin "The Kings Head Hotel was across the street and run by three sisters, all single. The elder was Miss Maud who was just an ordinary down-to-earth person. Miss Trixie was so dressy and wore her fair hair piled high and always had little bows of ribbon clipped in. Miss Edith was very funny to us children as she had her hair out like a man, was cross-eyed and walked with a roll. Their name was Outlaws. They employed an ostler named Juby Cook who went every day on the Spout Hills for a big can of water from the spout of the Hill spring."

ith Pointin "Alfred Lee s a dear old man and had ousekeeper named Miss oper. My mother always essed his chickens etc., d when I took them back always said to Miss oper, "Give the child a pence extra for herself."

There was a saddler, Luke Basham, opposite Rounce and Wortley (formerly Reliance Printing Works).

The Manor House was the home of Culley, who owned the shop next to the Feathers (see Chapter Five). Apparently he went bankrupt. The Preston photo shows his delivery cart disappearing down a huge crater, as a result of the horrendous downpour on August 26th 1912.

In the late twenties, Manor House became a preparatory school, Start Point, which will feature in the next volume.

rt Point Preparatory School, HOLT.

Mrs. F. A. SPENCER, B.A., F.R.G.S.
assisted by
Miss E. M. BYFORD, Matron
(S. Anne's College, Cheltenham)
Mr. J. V. HOWGATE.

BURROUGHES MILL 1792

THE FAIRSTEAD

Footpath to the Little Hills

← Home of the Williamson family

WINN'S NURSERY

ALFRED PAYNE carriages

BOARD SCHOOL

NEW

CROSS STREET

QUEEN ADELAIDE PH

WESLEYAN CHAPEL 1838

EMPSONS

STREET

CONCERT HALL
until mid 1920s
then cinema behind
co-op shop until 1937

Edith Pointin's home
LITERARY INSTITUTION

CHAPTER THREE

ALFRED LEE'S
then PURDY'S
bake shop
then BRIGG'S

HIGH STREET

Chapter 3

New Street

School's out, on an autumn afternoon – long shadows. On the right is Barclays Bank, with the front door to the Manager's residence. Then comes the Literary Institute, looking trim behind a low wall and railings. Much of the high wall beyond is still standing.

The fact that New Street is straight is as much a clue to its relative youth as its name! A study of maps in David Durst's collection shows its existence in the Tithe map of 1839, but not in Bryants, 1826. In *Three Centuries of Holt*, Jane Hales says its construction was begun around 1830; further, the deeds to a house in the town end of the street date from 1830. We must be very close to pinpointing the date of its construction! In its early years it was named as Withers Street, after a prominent local figure, who owned land here. According to Earle Kirby, whose childhood home was just off it and who ran his business on it as an adult, 'it's the coldest street in Holt.' Its straight line on the north-south axis may have something to do with that.

Alfred Lee's young employees pause between errands.

Starting at the junction with the High Street, we'll now step north and look at buildings to the right and left. On the corner in the early years of the century was one of Alfred Lee's two retail premises. This was followed by Purdy's bake house and shop, where the ovens were made available for housewives to bring some of their own cooking. Dora Hills can remember 'housewives going with cloth-covered trays'. Briggs later took over this business. Further up on the left is Lee's Terrace, which Jane Hales tells us was 'converted from an old pop factory at the end of last century'. Perhaps it was part of the premises bought by Morgans from Edward Carter Cooper (see Chapter Two), but surplus to requirements. On the right hand corner of the High Street stood the large, heavy edifice of Barclays Bank, followed immediately by a long, gracious building set behind a low brick wall, with iron railings.

The Literary Institution/Institute

This was founded in 1854 to provide a place in town where there were books available to borrow, and which provided newspapers and periodicals for members to read. It was on land belonging to what is now Barclays Bank, so it is likely that it was originally a charitable foundation given to the town by the syndicate of landowning families who set up the bank. Its opening hours were given each year in the Almanack. It was open every day in the year, except Sundays, Good Friday and Christmas Day, from nine in the morning until ten at night. That indicates a substantial commitment to serve the town. However, a newspaper feature which appeared in 1954 to mark its centenary tells of years of financial struggle to keep it open in the face of limited income. The intention was to finance it through subscriptions, but very often the management committee had to appeal for money from well-wishers, and/or fund-raising events. Rooms were available for hire, too, for various public gatherings. The feature article ends on rather a downbeat note:

railings have gone, the
sts remain. Probably near
end of its days.

th terms were in use.

The room is conveniently situated in New Street, Holt, and while of course it has its limitations, it does still endeavour to provide facilities during the day and some evenings for the perusal of carefully selected daily newspapers, weekly periodicals and monthly magazines and can be useful to visitors to the town who require somewhere to pass a short while, while making business or shopping visits to the town. The 'family' subscription is one guinea per year with other rates for various categories of members, obtainable from the secretary, Capt T Slator, Cromer Road, Holt. It seems that in these days of stress and strain, a sober institution such as the Literary Institute is not one to throw over lightly, and if the committee could be assured of a much larger measure of support from the town and district then improvements of facilities of the room could be entertained.

The Institute finally closed a year later and was demolished in the early sixties. The land is now the Barclays Bank car park.

A Holt Childhood – Edith Pointin

Edith wrote down her memories late in life, and they were passed to us for inclusion in this book. As always with material of this kind, the writing follows a particularly strong pulse of memory – whatever the topic! Edith ranges far and wide.

I was born at 8, New Street, on January 11th 1908. My father, Mr Robert Pels White, was born in 1874; my mother's name was Rosa White (née Wright). I was the youngest of five children. Tom Preston had a shop next door to us in New Street. He took photographs, framed pictures, and taught music.

When I was three years old I had whooping cough; it was so bad, the doctor said it was the worst case he'd ever had. I was having a real old cough in the garden, when a gypsy looked over the gate. I can picture her now. She said to Mother, 'What you want is new shoots of elder. Boil them, and give three glassfuls a day.' So off went my sister Lillian with me and a basket up Chapel Yard where shops have been built into the old houses, to Granny White's garden, which was surrounded by elder hedge. Mother made the drink and I got better – but it did taste nasty. We played with skipping-ropes, hoops, marbles, stilts and hopscotch as there was very little traffic. We children used to love it when a flock of sheep came through, also herds of cattle as there was quite a good cattle sale on Fridays up the Feathers yard.

A religious upbringing

We were always taught to say our prayers and grace, before meals and after, and to have only what you can call your own. Children didn't seem to get into trouble as parents were always at home when children got back from school – or mothers were, anyway. Most children went to Sunday School. There was St Andrew's church, the Wesleyan Chapel up New Street, which is now St. John's Hall, the United Church at the top of Letheringsett Hill, and the small Primitive Methodist Chapel in Back Street. This was later the Fire Station. My sister Annie and I went first of all to the United Church. We always loved Sunday School. I was three years old when I first went and Annie was five. The heating was under the floor, and it was lovely to walk along that part on a cold day. We had an Anniversary Sunday in the summer, when children said recitations to the public; the collections paid for a lovely party at Christmas, when we got books as prizes for regular attendance and good behaviour. My first book was called *The Stolen Roses*, dated December 1912. I kept it as new until my grandchildren tore it up. I still have one which I managed to retrieve in time; it is dated 1914. Later, we went to the Wesleyan Chapel. Every Sunday, Annie and I used to visit Granny White in Chapel Yard. This row of cottages are now shops mostly for antiques.

Family pastimes

My father played games each night with us in winter time until eight o'clock. Ludo, Snakes and Ladders, Tiddly Winks, draughts. I well remember my first game, Ludo – which I lost. I screamed and 'put on my parts', as they would say. I was only three years old, but remember Daddy saying, 'You cannot expect to win. Sometimes you win and sometimes you lose and you must not get upset. You must always play the game right.' These words have stuck in my memory.

Reading was always what I enjoyed – poetry especially, and I still remember poems I said at Sunday School anniversaries. Sunday School treats happened once a year, even if it were a picnic on Muckleburgh Hill at Weybourne or in a field at Letheringsett or going to a hall in Sheringham where we had jellies, cakes, etc.

New friends

The Cockaday family moved to Holt from

Norwich about this time and lived on Weston Square. My dad and Mr Cockaday started with racing pigeons. The days the pigeons were due back we were not allowed in the garden. My sister Lillian would have to run to the Railway Hotel to clock in when the pigeons returned. We had to go up a ladder to the loft where we loved seeing the young pigeons.

Sunday walks

On Sundays after dinner Mother and Daddy took us for walks according to the amount of time we had. There were many lovely walks as traffic was almost non-existent. Walks were:

1. Around Cley Watering, down Cley Road, turn left where the ford went across the road, right round to Letheringsett and home.

2. Round the two bridges up Cromer Road. Alas, one bridge has gone. Up to Brian Bullen's corner, turn left and along High Kelling to the other bridge and then along Kelling Road and home.

3. Round Selbrigg. We would go up the Hempstead Road, turn left before Hempstead and go round to the lake, where there were two swans, go along to Cromer Road, then home.

4. Round Holt Lowes. We would go up the Edgefield Road and just before Edgefield Hill, go through a gate. There was a lovely path with gorse and broom bushes each side, and of course, acres of lovely heathers. There were lots of pine trees round a pond and in the woods on the left side were masses of all sorts of wild orchids and other wild flowers. We eventually came out on the Hempstead Road to go home.

5. Round Runton Pore/Poor. This too was a lovely walk. We would start off going up the Thornage Road and turn off towards a small wood called Runton Pore/Poor. This we would bypass and go along to a railway line. There were stiles to cross over and then small paths across Mr Hubert Ellis' farm fields. We would come out at the beginning of Little Thornage where there was a small ford across the road. We would then go through part of Letheringsett and then home.

6. If we had only a short walk it would be what we called 'Round the Candlestick', going up Thornage Road to just before the Runton Pore turn. We would then come out on the Hunworth Road.

Every Sunday, weather permitting, my mother and father took my sister Annie and me on these walks. It was lovely. My pet name from many of mother's old relatives was 'The Little Wildflower Gatherer', as I just loved them and knew all their names. I think I knew where every wild flower grew around Holt, and I would be there as soon as I knew they would be out.

Edith tells of the importance to her of Brownies and Guides

Miss Joyce Reid and Miss May Culley ran the first Holt Girl Guides. My sister Annie was in that troop, but at that time I was not old enough. I joined the Brownies run by Mrs King at Holt Rectory until I was old enough to go to Miss Reid's Guides. It was great to go on marches singing along the country roads and to big rallies when we would have to march past royalty and Lady Baden-Powell, Lady Hastings, etc. We went to Melton Constable Hall many times, but the one I remembered most was at Massingham when the Princess Royal (Mary) came and walked along and spoke to each patrol. My sister Annie was Patrol Leader, and had a lovely fair-haired pigtail with a black bow, and the Princess

THE LOWES

stopped and touched my sister's hair, saying what a wonderful pigtail. The old Queen Mary was there also, but she stood aside. There were thousands of guards there; it was a wonderful day as we went in one of Mr Empson's wagonettes. We did morse code signalling with flags and were so proud of our uniforms, lanyards, badges, etc. And for the boys, Mr Ronnie Byford ran a big pack of scouts.

Edith reflects on her early life.

Life in Holt was good. There was no sex taught in schools, and as far as I know we children did not know about sex. We knew there was a difference but did not know what it entailed and I do not remember girls getting pregnant so life was carefree and innocent. We children had to say grace before and after meals, also kneel and say our prayers before getting into bed. I well remember on cold nights, 'Can't we say it in bed beside a lovely stone hot water bottle?' There were no radios, electric lights and gas stoves I guess, as I never saw any in the houses I knew. Children did as they were told.

The family ran a bakery, too. Note the advertising between the windows at first-floor level.

Walter and Ben Empson

This fine photo shows the carriage of Walter Empson outside his home in New Street the southern side of the Wesleyan Chapel. Walter himself is at the reins, with members of his family aboard. Next to him in front is his daughter Maud, while his six or seven year old son Ben is just behind the lamp. Ben was born in 1900, so we may date this as 1906/7. He is just a lad

here, but in the nineteen twenties, he was already working in the family carrier business which he took over, on his father's death, in 1928. He operated from these premises in New Street, too; behind the house there was a range of stables which later became the base of his prestigious riding establishment. But we advance too far! Ben is also remembered for other qualities. Here, one of the King daughters, Beatrice, recalls a journey in the Empson carriage in the dark.

ree friends, with button-
les, take time out together.
know two of them,
lter Empson and
lter Horne.

Parties in the big houses were on a very grand scale, with tables groaning with gorgeous cakes and jellies and crackers. Very often one had a lovely present at the end. One memorable party for me was in a village beyond Letheringsett. It took place after dark. We had to go in Ben Empson's carriage and got stuck in the ford which we had to cross. Ben Empson was a big, handsome man – a big heart-throb – and he always wore beautifully-polished riding-boots. Well, he had to get out and persuade the horses to go on, and I thought of him getting very wet feet and spoiling those lovely boots. But equally, I was a little scared as we were in party frocks and light party shoes, and afraid of having to get out and wade in the water. However, Ben got them moving. It was all very exciting and romantic. Years later I found that the ford was only an inch or two deep, no great hazard really. But in the dark, how was I to know that?

n's daughter Mary was
ly five years old when her
her died, but this story
s often told her by her
)ther.

Mrs Empson "Ben used to drive for a family named Pope, who lived in Wansbeck House in the twenties. They were rather a posh, proper pair, with a son away at Eton. He particularly remembered one breakfast he shared with them, where boiled eggs were served. The son, who was quite young at the time, chopped the top off his egg, went as to eat it, tried it – but then thought better of the idea. Said father, very Victorian and stern, looking over the top of his glasses, 'C'm on, boy, eat up!' – to which the boy replied, 'Sorry, I don't fancy it.' 'What do you mean, you don't fancy it!' To which came the reply, 'Well, I think it's slightly incubated, papa!'"

The Concert Hall

The photo on the left dates from the thirties, and it is the only one to come to light showing the premises of the Norwich Co-operative Society shop, which was set up a few years earlier. It is chiefly remembered now for the cinema which lay behind the shop, in what had been the Concert Hall, owned up till then by Arthur Preston of the printing-works. The story of the cinema belongs to the next volume, with many accounts of happy Saturday matinees. A closer look at the photo reveals the letters CIN just above an entrance beyond the shop

Betty Mann "There was a Concert Party called the Sunflowers who entertained people there; both my cousin and I learned the piano, and they asked us to play duets for them. We were never separated, hardly, as kids."

Two reports from the Holt Almanacks.

Jane Hales The old concert hall (Preston's hall) was a coach-builders, Battrick, at one time.

The congregation of the Wesleyan chapel in the early twenties.

window. This opened into a passage which led through to a building at the back. The map shows this to have been at right angles to the street, but we're unlikely to find out a great deal more about it as it burnt down in 1937. In its day, the Concert Hall provided a venue for many kinds of entertainment. Betty Mann remembers playing the piano there with her cousin.

10 February 1910. The annual Stewards' Ball took place. The Concert Hall has rarely presented so beautiful an appearance, the place being transformed. Between seventy and eighty accepted the invitation and dancing was pursued with vigour until the early hours of the morning. Much of the success of the evening was due to the excellent work put in by the Hon Secretaries, Messrs G Cooke and L Knowles. Mr Cooke was also MC and was indefatigable in his endeavours to secure a successful evening.

27 January 1915. The third Patriotic Smoker arranged by the Holt Unionist Association was held in the Concert Hall, and was well attended by members of the Association, and of His Majesty's Forces stationed in the district. Dr RT Hales was in the chair, and in the course of a few remarks, stated what pleasure it gave the Unionist Association to arrange these concerts, not only for their own members, but for their military friends. An excellent programme had been arranged, and was keenly appreciated by those present.

The Wesleyan Chapel

The Wesleyan Methodists worshipped here for the first three decades of the century, before all strands of Methodism amalgamated in 1932. In her study of Methodism in Holt, Elizabeth Bellamy says this of those early years:

The three Methodist Churches continued side by side through to the first third of the twentieth century. There is no real evidence of any contact between them, nor of any antipathy either. Each related to a circuit of its own denomination and through it to its own annual Conference and Connexional structures. Each was served by ministers of its own. At the turn of the century, Holt was still a circuit in its own right of the Wesleyan Conference with one minister, presumably resident in the town. The Primitive Methodists were in the Holt and Sheringham Circuit, with two ministers, one living in Holt. The Free Methodists were part of the Holt Free Methodist Circuit with one minister. Each church had its own choir, Sunday School, meetings, fundraising events and anniversaries, as well as the services, class meetings and annual specials.

The Board School

This school, now the Dyson & Faircloth garage, was built in 1851 at the expense of WH Cozens-Hardy, a man who played a leading role in the nineteenth century in Holt. We have already met the name in connection with the complex history of Methodism in the town, and the school was originally a Methodist foundation, the British Schoolroom. Indeed, when the Wesleyan Reformers split from the Wesleyans in the middle of the century, they first used these school premises as their chapel. Subsequently it acquired the name 'The Board School' a name that survived, although it was re-styled as 'Council School' in its closing years. Education continued here until 1928, when the new school buildings in Norwich Road opened on land next to the Infants School. For a period of nearly eighty years, then, this building was central to the lives of many Holt children. And for over half of those years, its Head Master was Mr Hutchens.

king due south down
v Street, the Board
ool (now the garage
on and Faircloth) to the
The Queen Adelaide pub
rther down on the right.

Looking at the size of the building today, and the small plot of land it occupies, it is astonishing that these premises could contain the number of children on roll – no less than 274 in December 1902, for example. No wonder Mr Hutchens found it difficult to fulfil the requirements for physical education as laid down in the manuals of the government of the day – one of the regular areas for comment we may read in the School Log. This tome was updated on a weekly basis by the Head Master, and provides an insight into some of the day by day issues confronting him. It also incorporates copies of HMI reports following inspections every few years.

A reading of this log soon makes it very clear that the premises were problematic throughout. In common with other schools at this period, too, children's health was often a major factor affecting attendance. There are frequent references to diphtheria, measles, scarlatina (scarlet fever), mumps and other ailments. Not to mention the difficulties that bad weather brought (travelling conditions, lack of fuel for heating) and the regular disruption to studies caused by the pupils' involvement with harvest.

Portrait of Hutchens (above) and at his front door (below).

Henry Hobart "After that I went to the Board School, Mr Bramley was the head master there, and there was a Mr Bond, too - they used to hit pupils with a ruler, you know, they did that. I can tell you one instance, I've seen parents go in there, one lady, Mrs R. – she was about six feet high and six feet across – she came in once to see Mr Bond, and threaten him, 'Don't you touch my boys again!' And another time, I saw Bramley take two boys into the lobby, W. and K. they were called, he was going to hit these boys with his stick – well those boys were almost as big as him, they took the stick off him and thrashed him with it instead! But he never reported them! They got away with it."

Order is good and instruction is generally effective though the children might with advantage be trained to work more on their own account. The managers should at once take steps to procure a suitable place for physical training which cannot be properly be carried out in the school premises and the requirements of Schedule 3 of the Provisional Code are not satisfied. (HMI report 1903)

The severe overcrowding that was clearly evident when the above report was written must have been alleviated in 1910 by the opening of the Infants School in Norwich Road. However, shortage of space was still a problem! The Inspector's report of 1911 states the problem quite graphically:

The only playground available for the physical training of the 136 children in this school is a small yard, fifteen yards by six and a half yards exposed to the road. The playground is not asphalted and when the school was visited the children were so choked with dust that the lesson had to be abandoned.

Mr Hutchens closed his career at the Board School on Monday, August 3rd 1914, the day before the First World War broke out. Overall, the log reveals him to have been a conscientious man, if somewhat self-important. He allows himself occasional admissions of comparative failure, but compensates these with regular bouts of self-congratulation. Sadly, his period of retirement was to prove very brief. We read the following entry in the Almanack for 1915.

3 February 1915. The death has occurred with painful suddenness of Mr Francis T Hutchens. He was taken ill whilst in the Literary Institute, of which he was Secretary. Dr RT Hales was immediately summoned, but Mr Hutchens passed away within half an hour, his death being ascribed to cerebral haemorrhage. The deceased gentleman had left his house apparently in his usual state of health, and the news of his death and its tragic nature was the topic of talk in Holt during the day, and much sympathy was expressed for the bereaved family.

His successor was an appointee from Nottingham, Mr John Bramley, who took over in trying wartime conditions, with constant difficulties over supplies of coal for the classroom stoves. Again, in his report of December 1916, the Inspector highlights the poor teaching conditions:

The need for improved accommodation here is urgent, and should be considered as soon as circumstances permit. The playground is totally inadequate, the heating and ventilation

...dley Bond, a keen bowls ...yer when not in the ...ssroom.

...inspector's report ...mmented: 'The second ...ss contains an abnormal ...mber of retarded children. ...s taught by a most consci-...ous uncertificated ...cher who suffered ...erely during the war... ...is not strong enough ...ysically to cope with the ...iculties of this important ...up.'

...el Potter "We all liked ...headmaster we had at ...w Street, but he had to ...He was a Mr Bramley ...m Nottingham. He always ...d us that if we took the ...n to Nottingham we ...uld see the Castle quite ...inly, which I found to be ...e later on. There was also ...Mr Bond, a Holt man, who ...s a newspaper reporter as ...ll, and a Miss White and a ...ss Payne. I don't know ...ere they came from. ...at's all I can remember, ...t I know that the old ...ool in New Street turned ...t some clever pupils under ...Bramley."

and office (toilet) and cloakroom arrangements are highly unsatisfactory, and the premises generally very inconvenient. The defective ventilation of the main room requires immediate attention.

The name of a man associated with Holt in many areas, including his work as a teacher, enters the log for the first time on March 3rd 1919 – that of Mr Hedley Bond, when he commenced duties as an uncertificated assistant. He is often reported as being absent in ensuing years. His reliance on the hard edge of a ruler as a disciplinary tool was legendary, and often the subject of comment by pupils who remember life in his classroom. But they conceded, too, that this habit could be attributed to ongoing health problems as a result of injuries sustained in the First World War.

In October 1920 gardening was introduced to the curriculum, an innovation which the pupils must have warmly welcomed – if only as an excuse to flee the four walls of the classroom. But as for Mr Bramley, he had more problems to endure, this time for lack of teacher cover when staff were unwell. The next HMI reports that 'The Headmaster was responsible for teaching 80 children in two classes as well as for the supervision of the school for four consecutive months.'

However, a small crumb of comfort comes in the HMI report of November 29th 1927, which acknowledges the effort put in. 'During the last three years the Head Master has striven to improve the condition of this school, but his efforts have not met with the success they deserved.' And the report ends with: 'The teaching power does not appear to be adequate for a school of this size. There is a felt need especially for an experienced woman teacher to take an effective part in the education of the older girls.'

But perhaps we have relied too much on official reports. One of the pupils smiling in the photo overleaf is Ethel Potter (née Everitt), who retains a very positive view of her old Head Master. He did his job well and he was a man of his word – what is more important to a child than that?

So, eventually, after years of struggling with poor conditions, and with many staff who were neither trained nor particularly fit, Mr J Bramley stepped down as Head Master in 1928. He was not appointed to be Head of the new school in Norwich Road. But other circumstances, unearthed by one adroit sleuth on the Holt History Project team, Terry Thacker, may have played their part here... We shall return to the matter later!

Clifford Watts introduces his classmates, and gives the occupation of the father, where he can remember.

1 Tom Bane – agricultural labourer

2 Leslie Hobart – worker in Platten stone pits

3 Clifford Watts – railway worker

4 Arthur Randell – agricultural labourer

5 Alfred Moy – agricultural labourer, Letheringsett

6 Archie Middleton – agricultural labourer, worked for Burroughes, who owned the mill, on their land.

7 Joe Pope – employee with Pratt's petrol

8 Mabel Spalding – painter/decorator

9 Ethel Everitt – unknown

10 Wilcox – pastry cook, New Street

The Board School closes 1928

This is a class photo from 1928, the year the education authorities discontinued running a school on these premises in New Street. The school had already changed its name to Council School, as the placard being held up by the boy in the foreground, indicates – 'Holt Council School, 1928'. The new building on the Norwich Road opened later in the same year. After closing as a school, this building was used as an egg depot. And here's a remarkable feat of recall: one of the boys in the back row, Clifford Watts (3), was

11 Dorothy Starling, journeyman, delivery cart for Byfords.

12 Grace Beresford – market gardener, Kelling Road

13 Marjorie Wright – publican at the Paul Pry

14 Scott – gasworker

15 Joan Wolsey – handyman

16 Eileen Platten – postman

17 Archie Checkley – builder's labourer

18 Molly Beresford – unknown

19 Marjorie / Mary Gaelor – unknown

20 Kathleen Platten (sister to Eileen) – postman

21 Evelyn Crowe – builder's labourer

22 Rose Allen – unknown

23 Allen (sister)

24 Betty King – unknown

25 Kitchener (?) Walpole – Head Gardener, Kelling Sanatorium

26 Peter Turner – Postmaster, Letheringsett PO

27 Cyril Hall – ex-patient at Kelling Sanatorium, stayed on as employee.

28 Freddie Crowe – builder's labourer

29 Kenneth Swann – gardener to Rvd Upcher of Shrublands

able to give me both Christian and surnames of all but four of the twenty-nine pupils, and the occupation of the fathers of most of them, in October 2004 – seventy-six years later! Doubtless they were a very special group to him – after all, they included the girl who became his wife in 1939, Dorothy Starling (11). They have had five children, twelve grandchildren and four great-grandchildren – so far! Sadly, Dorothy died in the nineteen eighties.

Clifford's final comment on his classmates: When we left school, we were lucky to get a job at all. I did all right, though, I went into carpentry.

Archie Checkley

Archie Checkley

We are all in this little boy's debt. Here he is in a school photo, standing slightly apart from his fellows, very smartly dressed, with a searching gaze towards the lens. Perhaps even in those days he was enthralled by the consequence of the cameraman's click. Archie was to work in the town all his life (except for war years), starting as delivery boy in the newsagent's shop belonging to Rounce and Wortley, and ending his career as manager there. From an early age he collected photos and memorabilia to do with Holt. Many early photos of the town were produced for the postcard trade, and although of only passing value at that stage, they became, in due course, treasured items in their own right. Throughout his life, Archie was a significant collector, gathering all his findings in huge albums, which he delighted in showing people. It was always his intention that his collection would pass one day to a Holt Museum; in the meantime they are in the custody of the Norfolk Record Office. His is not the only collection I have used in the course of compiling this book, but I would not have been able to dub it 'An Illustrated History of Holt' without access to his albums. Thank you, Archie. Your lifelong passion for your town has immeasurably enriched our knowledge of its history.

Alfred Payne

It is always intriguing to learn of splendid achievements in craftsmanship in areas that have now become obsolete, and the carriage-works of Alfred Payne are one such example. We know that, sadly, most of the family records were discarded years ago, so we will probably have to content ourselves with the odd document and a few memories. But in its prime, it was evidently an outstanding operation, serving clients from the landed gentry and the farming community. Just recall the list of vehicles in common use given to us by Francis King, on page 39. From accompanying descriptions we can say that the work was carried out on both sides of New Street. The photo here is of the carriage outside a glazed roadside workshop. This lies on the right as we leave town, just beyond the house where Alfred lived with his family. After Payne ceased trading in the late thirties, it was taken over by the building firm of Cockaday. On the other side was a long L-shaped building, where 'they used to put tyres on wheels' (Cliff Watts), and do the preliminary construction work on the vehicles. This in its turn became the workshop of Earle Kirby's Holt Cellulosing Company, in the years after the Second World War. The main building we see in the photo was the finishing shop.

Cliff Watts "The Paynes were tip-top people, they wouldn't let anything go out with a scratch or anything like that. They were master people, they really were."

Charles E Winn

Charles E Winn was born in Baconsthorpe in 1877; his father John William Winn was a local Methodist preacher for 56 years, a farm steward, and a very prominent figure in local affairs. Charles trained as journeyman gardener on various estates in England and Scotland; he met his future wife Mary on the Earl of Stairs' estate in East Lothian, where she worked as dairymaid. They married and moved to Cirencester, where their first two children were born. Their move back to Norfolk came in 1906, when they acquired Garden Cottage (said to be the oldest house in New Street), and the nursery garden. Clearly a man of energy and enterprise, Charles developed his business here, where his grand-daughter Gillian Barwick reports:

ALFRED PAYNE,
(Late Vines and Payne),
COACH BUILDER, &c.,
NEW STREET, HOLT.
Carriages of every description built to order.
ESTIMATES GIVEN FOR REPAIRS.

As well as tomato and cucumber houses there was a magnificent black grape vine, and a fern house heated to a very humid atmosphere. A cooler extension of this grew freesias and other tender flowers as well as pot plants and exotics such as pineapples and palms, then unobtainable in country districts, except direct from Covent Garden. Grandfather himself sent a lot of his own produce to Covent Garden.' He became a Fellow of the Royal Horticultural Society, and was chairman of Holt Horticultural Society.

Business prospered, and his family grew, eventually to seven children. He bought a larger house behind the nursery, at the top of Letheringsett Hill, whose land adjoined his existing property in New Street. His wife Mary named her house Soutra, in memory of the landscape surrounding her family home in Scotland.

As well as his thriving business and family life, Charles Winn was very active in local affairs. He was at one time Chairman of the Parish Council, he represented Holt on Erpingham RDC, and he was involved with the Playing Field Committee, the Housing Committee, and the Old Folk's Club. Like his father, he became a Methodist Lay Preacher, initially at the Wesleyan Chapel in New Street, and subsequently for the Holt Methodist Free Church on Obelisk Plain. Gillian Barwick describes him as being a 'stern Victorian father'! His wife Mary was equally committed to their faith – her obituary (1944) states: 'From 1922–1933 she rendered faithful and exemplary service in the Wesleyan Church, New Street, as leader of a Young People's Fellowship, and at amalgamation of Methodism, she continued at Norwich Road Methodist Church as vice-president of the Sisterhood.

We shall return to the Winn family in our next volume.

C. E. WINN,

Fruiterer, Florist, Seedsman, etc.

NEW STREET, HOLT

WREATHS, CROSSES, BOUQUETS &c.

From 3/6, 5/6, 10/6, 15/- and upwards, made to order with pure White Flowers. This is our Speciality.

The Largest Growers of Bedding Plants in the Neighbourhood.

Estimates Given for Landscape Gardening.
——Fruit Trees.   Shrubs Supplied.——
Thoroughly Practical in every branch of Gardening.

The Williamson Family

Amazingly, all the babies, toddlers, children, and young adults pictured opposite are the family of one set of parents, Maude and Albert Williamson. Here are the statistics: there were nineteen in all, two of whom died in infancy. The seventeen who survived – and thrived – comprised two sets of twins, the girl twins arriving before the boys. Maude and Albert's first-born was a daughter, Violet, born in 1904, and the youngest, Monica, in 1926. For many years the family lived in Hill Cottage, a small house set on the Little Hills, but accessible to New Street by a footpath, which is still in use. The family later moved to Albert Street. We in the Holt History Project had heard of the family in the course of our researches, but we met up through another remarkable fact. Our exhibition in April, 2004 opened on the hundredth anniversary of Violet's birth, and her own son Jack (just a year younger than his aunt Monica!) returned to Holt to lay flowers on his mother's grave – and looked in to see us. In conversation later, it transpired that there are three surviving children from the original family. Jack put me in touch with his uncle Jimmy, born in 1918. We should add a few words about their house. It comprised two bedrooms upstairs, a larger one and a small one, with downstairs a living-room, a small kitchen and a pantry. There was no electricity and no water, and there was a dry lavatory. Water had to be collected in buckets from an outside tap which was situated by the cottages near the gasworks – a considerable trek beyond

t Buxton (née King) They
ere a wonderful, happy
mily who we visited
casionally, I believe, to
ss on clothes etc. (These
d already been passed on
us from wealthy friends of
e parents in London. I
member particularly being
mazed to see the small
ildren quite happily eating
w potatoes. Even in those
ys, when we were so well
d, it seemed sad, but as
ey were apparently so
ntent, I was told to be
ankful for that.

Letheringsett Road. A few years later, in the early thirties, water was piped to them from the Fairstead. Jimmy spoke with great warmth of his family and upbringing.

Jimmy Williamson "We had wonderful parents, my mother was an incredible woman, and my dad had the patience of Job – he was a wonderful man. He was originally from Fakenham, and worked as a signalman. He had a big allotment down by the railway. My mother's maiden name was Bolton, and her family had lived in a railway carriage up the Hempstead Road. As for the sleeping arrangements – well, remember, there was a large age gap between eldest and youngest, so there was probably only ten or twelve of us living at home at any one time. My parents slept in the smaller room upstairs, leaving the larger bedroom for the rest of us! There was one large double bed in there, with four of us at one end and four at the other. Those that were left slept on the other bed. We younger boys used to go round to the Burroughes house – the miller, in New Street – to do odd jobs, like stoking the boiler, cleaning shoes, running errands, chopping wood. One morning, I chopped the top of my thumb off, so I've had only half a thumb for most of my life. Once they left school, at fourteen, most of the girls went into service, some living in at their workplace in Holt, some going away."

Edith Pointin The Williamson's cottage was spotless. The father was only a signalman at the station, and there was no child allowance. Mrs Williamson would go and sit on the Hills with lots of the children, and my friends and I would go too. We were great friends, us children, not wanting the moon.

Jane Hales At the northern extremity, the Fairstead Row marked the end of the building till after the 1914–18 war, when the first Council Estate was put up on the Fairstead itself. The houses are of mixed flint and brick, the most pleasing effort so far on the part of the Authority.

Cliff Watts "I can remember going down to the Fairstead, when they'd started to put the houses there, at the age of eight or nine. All the foundations were dug out, pick and shovel, no digger! They were beautiful, we'd go down there and run round them – there were frogs everywhere!"

The Fairstead
A Holt Childhood – Earle Kirby

Earle Kirby's family was one of the first to move into the new houses at the Fairstead. He gives us an insight into his eventful childhood.

Earle Kirby "My dad moved us into a little cottage right next to the mill, and he put his name down for one of the new council houses on the Fairstead, built I believe in 1921, and he was the first one to move in. There's a little path that runs behind the houses – I used to come out of my garden, down the path and straight on to the Little Hills – and that's where my life was."

School life

"When I was first put to school, it was at the new Infants School; my first day, I went off, it was a Monday, wash day for my mother, and at eleven o'clock she saw me come back. 'What are you doing here?' 'Oh, I said, it's all over, it's finished.' 'No, it's not, it doesn't finish till three o'clock.' 'Well, I've finished,' I replied. Anyway, Miss Bunkell arrived at the door, on her bike. 'Do you think we can get him back if we let him ride his trike?' And that's how they managed to cajole me back to school! I enjoyed my time there, but then I started up at the Board School in New Street, and I hated every minute of that – I was very unhappy there; then my parents, being church people, put me to the Church School, at the age of seven or eight. It was a lovely old school, with about ninety-five pupils. The Head Master was called Mr Mould, and we were very happy there; I made a lot of friends. Going to school from the Fairstead where we lived, I went every day via the Little Hills. The school was a distinctive little building, opposite what was then the Carpenters Arms. Of course there was the new state school just built down the road, and there was great rivalry between the schools. In wintertime, when the other children had to come past ours to get to theirs, we used to have great snowball fights. I was always happy there, I became a member of football and cricket teams, we had to cycle to our matches, we weren't carried about in cars. We went to Briston, Hindolveston – but oh dear, we got into some muddle if we won – we got chased out of the village!

Living on the Fairstead

"One thing – I can actually remember the names of the fourteen original occupants of the Fairstead, which is a beautifully laid out estate. Here we go: the Gilberts; the Houchens; Arthur Lewis, the footballer, his dad; our family; the Kirbys at number 4; Charlie Stavely, insurance man, Number 6; Mr Shipp, the cycle agent; Pope in the corner; this is the one that gets me, Pells, I think; Dady Woodrow in the corner – a lot of controversy whether he should run a business from a council house, the usual thing; postman called Bainger Thorndyke; Mr Sheldrake, the radio man; the Spenlows, I was friends with the two boys; the Jarrolds; then the Sparks. I may be wrong, but that's reasonably correct. But soon after, they built the Legion houses down the Cley Road, the Spenlows moved down there, he was an ex-soldier.

When we lived just behind the Little Hills, there used to be a little man with a horse and cart, who came round; he had all stone jars on the cart, jars of Sasperella. When you bought the first jar, you had to buy that and the contents, but after that you just paid for the refill. It was lovely, I think it was the forerunner of Coca Cola, really, because that was the taste I remember. I think he came from down Wells way. There was the old 'Stop me and buy one!' who used to come up our little place. And Walls' ice-creams – they used have men go round with a big box arrangement on their cycle, a kind of cool-box."

Boys, stones and gas-lamps

"In Shirehall Plain there's a little shop which now is Crowe's the grocers; as a boy, that was the gas showroom, managed by a gentleman called Mr Holt; his wife was a very large lady, and he was a very small man, both cockneys, lovely people, but he had this unfortunate habit of saying 'bleeding' as every other word. I can remember as a boy, down on the Fairstead, we'd throw stones – that was a common thing in those days, I'm afraid – that wouldn't be allowed today; anyway, we used to knock the glass out of the lamp standard. Mr Holt's daily job was going round Holt at dusk, lighting up the gas lamps; this he would do by riding on a bicycle with a ladder, whatever the weather. And then much later, at eleven o'clock, he'd go round again putting the lights out. Well, one particular day, he came down the Fairstead, put his ladder up on the lamppost, and started climbing up; when he got to the top, he saw all the glass was knocked out. Now, we boys were hidden up somewhere, looking out, and we heard him say: 'Who the bleeding hell done this?' He

Earle Kirby "My mother was a Londoner, born in Peckham, and her father was a shoemaker. She had one sister, married to Harry Hale, and they came to Holt for their holiday every year. They travelled by train, they'd walk down from the old railway station with their suitcases into Holt, and they'd go straight to Shipp's cycle shop (now Alliance & Leicester), where they'd pick up two cycles. They'd put their cases on these and walk up to the Fairstead. And then every day they'd go out cycling. They loved it. Now the first thing they did when they got to our house, was this: they'd take a bottle, they'd go across to the Hills, and they'd fill their bottle from the Spout."

came down his ladder, stomped round to all the houses to find out who the culprits were – there were lots of children living there at the time – and I got roped in with the blame!

And I can remember Gus and his bike on another occasion. He was cycling along with his ladder on his shoulder, minding his own business, when somebody hailed him, 'Hiya, Gus!', so round he swung, forgot about the ladder, nearly took the head off the man cycling behind him. 'Hey, Gus, whatever you think you're doing?' So Gus then swung the other way and nearly knocked the windscreen out of a car! Just like a routine in a comic film, you can imagine."

The Windmill

We are grateful to Gerald Cubitt for supplying the information contained in the following paragraph.

This brick-built smock mill dates from the late eighteenth century. When offered for sale in June, 1792, it was described as being 'a new erected windmill'. It had the following specification: there were four double-shuttered sails in eight bays of three; the cap was boat-shaped, with petticoat; the fan comprised eight blades; there were five floors in all, a gallery, and a stage at first-floor level. The last miller to work the mill solely by wind power was Sydney Stephen Burroughes, miller and general merchant, who bought it in 1896. It continued in use until about 1920, with steam power supplementing wind power in later years. The sails were taken down in the spring of 1922, while the rest of the machinery was removed in the early thirties. The brick tower was then used for storage, until the whole site was sold by the Burroughes family to AG Wright Ltd in January 1973. The tower was deemed to be unsafe by that time, and demolished later that year.

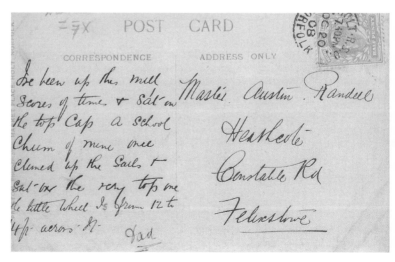

ODDFELLOWS HALL

ROUNCE and WORTLEY

DRILL HALL

pigeon loft

WATER TOWER

STREET

CHAPEL YARD

CROSS STREET

IKY'S FORGE

allotments

PRIMITIVE METHODIST CHAPEL built 1872

ALBERT

FRANKLIN'S YARD

WESTON SQUARE

BYFORD'S

I HOPE I DON'T INTRUDE

KNOWLES TAILORS workshop in PAUL PRY YARD

PAUL PRY INN

LEES YARD

built 1885 demolished 1950s

CHAPTER FOUR

SHIRE HALL PLAIN

TO THE BULL and Hanworth House

BULL STREET

SHIRE HALL

Chapter 4

Archibald Cockaday, photographed in the regalia of Grand Master of the Order of Oddfellows.

4 September 1910. A church parade organised by the local Alexander Lodge MU took place. The members attended at the Oddfellows Hall and marched through the principal streets. The Hindolveston brass band was in attendance. After parading the town, the procession wended its way to the Hills, where a service took place. The rector preached and dealt with the splendid work done by Friendly Societies.

8 September 1910. A series of Juvenile Sports under the auspices of the loyal Alexander Lodge of Oddfellows was held on the Fairstead. The sports were arranged among other events to mark the centenary year of the order, and proved to be most successful. After the sports, the juveniles adjourned to the Oddfellows Hall, where tea awaited them, and following which they were delighted and amused by delightful ventriloquial and conjuring entertainment given by Professor Balls of Sheringham.

Albert Street

Albert Street was the old Cley road before New Street was cut through. At the northern end stands a handsome building, now an Antiques Centre, which has played a major role in the life of the town. On the 1906 Ordnance Survey map this street is shown as Corn Hall Street – so that gives us an indication of its use at that point. In Peter Brook's succinct and informative booklet in the Poppyland series, he identifies it as originally a Calvinist church, sold in 1857 to become the corn exchange. The Salvation Army had the use of it on Saturday nights. Around the period of the First World War, it was known as the Town Hall, with the lessee a certain Mr CW Jex. Take note of that name, we'll meet Mr Sly-Jex (his full surname) again. In the years between the two World Wars the Town Hall housed the Ivy Leaf Club, the social centre for the British Legion. At a later point it became known as Oddfellows Hall as a result of its association with that organisation, a Friendly Society which was particularly active in Holt. Many of the cottages in this part of town were at one stage owned by the Oddfellows, and let to members.

Friendly Societies

In the 19th century, with no buffer against misfortune/poverty, prudent workers began to make monthly insurance payments into Friendly Societies, set up with the very purpose of providing for members in hard times. Small sums would be paid out in respect of funeral expenses and to replace wages when sickness struck. May 29th was the day each year when members celebrated their Societies with marches, church services and feasts. The passing of the National Health Insurance Act of 1911 gave a much reduced role to the Friendly Societies, and their importance in the social fabric steadily diminished.

Here is a list of Friendly Societies in the 1911 Holt Almanack. Each had its own board of trustees in the town.

> Reepham Provident Society
>
> Ancient Order of Foresters
>
> Pride of Holt Juvenile Friendly Society
>
> Holt District Manchester Unity IOOF
>
> Loyal Alexander Lodge
>
> Alexander Oddfellows Juvenile Friendly Society
>
> Independent Order of Rechabites
>
> Hope of Holt Lodge, No.45
>
> The Rational Association Friendly Society

The Allotments

The Allotment Gardens feature in the 1906 Ordnance Survey map. As well as serving the intended purpose of providing land for growing produce for those townspeople whose home had no garden, they accommodated pigeon lofts. Earle Kirby was employed by one of the regular race contestants.

Earle Kirby "As a boy of seven or eight, I used to run for Gussie Clarke who kept pigeons on his allotment near the mill. He wanted me because I could run so fast, and I did get him one or two results. The bird flew into his loft, he'd take the ring off, give it to me, and I'd run down to Sheldrake's, right down the back streets, I'd go like the wind, there was not much traffic about; I'd give it to Mr Sheldrake who'd put it in a capsule, then into the clock. There were several boys who were engaged as runners, like me – it could mean winning or losing. Sheldrake had the only clock in the town – a special thing where they put the rings in and the time was recorded, and nobody could cheat.

That was before Cockadays had the first individually-owned clock – so there was no need for anybody to run through the town. As I got older this gentleman gave me a pair of black pigeons – I was so proud of those, there weren't many people with black ones – which I kept on the Fairstead. I was taken once or twice to a meeting at the Railway Inn, and I got appointed secretary of the junior club. I sent a bird to San Sebastian in Spain, and I got him home; I didn't win anything, but I did get him home."

Rounce and Wortley

As we have seen, Arthur Preston sold the Reliance Printing Works, then situated on the High Street next to Barclays bank, to Rounce and Wortley. After the First World War, they re-located to Albert Street, taking advantage of a military building at the Weybourne camp which was surplus to requirements. This large wooden hut remained their premises until the firm closed in the 1980s – something of a bargain buy. However, we have to wonder at its suitability for a small industrial operation in view of fire risks, considering that it had pine flooring, and both its inner and outer walls were wooden, too. Not to mention the

money-raising float stands waiting outside premises of Rounce and Wortley. 1920s

Francis Wortley

Mabel Gotts "I used to go and sing in the concerts in the old Drill Hall. I always remember one song we sung – and I had to take the solo part of it and we were dressed up like the moons. 'Haven't you got the black moon way up there, I don't like the white moon shining, Every time I want to spoo-oo-oon, out there comes a big white moon! But we did have some good concerts."

Edith Pointin "Mr Gidney used the Drill Hall to use as a store for the rags, bones, rabbit skins he bought up. We would often take bones and get tuppence or threepence for rabbit skins – it all depended on the condition."

insulating material – sawdust! For many years, the foreman here was Russell Hunt, one of the apprentices standing in front of the High Street premises before the First World War. Russell, originally from Cromer, married Audrey Horne, daughter of Walter Horne, stone mason, of Obelisk Plain.

They settled in the town, spending the rest of their lives in Holt. Russell was as much interested in writing as in printing, contributing articles on town affairs to both the North Norfolk News and the EDP. Indeed, his familiarity with all aspects of the printed word led his daughter Mary Butcher, to say 'he could read across the room upside down.' He also shared one of the other passions of the town – bowls. Russell Hunt is another name to notice; we meet him in very different circumstances later.

The Drill Hall

If you wanted to hold a meeting in Holt in the first years of the

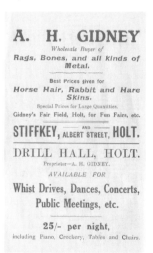

twentieth century, you had a very wide choice of venues: the Oddfellows Hall, the Drill Hall, the Shire Hall, the Church Hall; the Literary Institute, three chapels and ten public houses. This advertisement from the 1929 Holt Almanack identifies the owner of the Drill Hall at the time, and his trade. Which brings us to a gentleman by the name of Tent Nurse, who must have been a regular client over many years. In the course of our conversations with people with have long memories of Holt, this name kept recurring. Or was it Tenth Nurse?

Earle Kirby "Tenth Nurse was a poacher was a legendary figure, mysterious, he could trap rabbits, trap things. He had a reputation in the town."

The same man features in an article by the broadcaster Godfrey Winn, who visited Holt during the Second World War. Winn could not resist asking: 'How did you get such a curious Christian name?' The reply was not entirely conclusive. He was apparently born on the 10th of March in the year Prince Albert died. Or did his name derive from the fact that he was born on Prince Albert's birthday? He couldn't be sure. But whatever the reason, the name stuck. So did his reputation; he was 'acknowledged by all to be the best rabbit catcher living.'

Tent Nurse

This photo, taken in 1912, shows a line-up of Holt men. It serves to remind us of the very close connection between town and country in those years. With no traffic and no residential streets beyond the town itself (with the exception of Cromer Road), the country began everywhere just the other side of the wall, the hedge, the fence.

bel Gotts "He went to
er some boots to be
de, and when he came
ck a week later he asked
price. Two pounds ten,
s the answer. And Tent
d, Well, I can only give
fifty bob!" *(Shrieks of
ghter from the group.)*

rothy High "If you tell me
v many rabbits I've got in
sack, I'll give you the
ole seven."

The Yards

Of necessity, towns adapt to changing circumstances, but in the course of acquiring a car park, inner Holt lost some of its most characteristic housing. Chapel Yard takes its name from the Primitive Methodist Chapel. Franklin's Yard was 'named after a builder, who, with his wife, walked to Holt from Pembrokeshire, in the mid eighteenth century. Unfortunately this handsome yard was pulled down in 1967.' (Jane Hales.) Lees Yard is named after Alfred Lee, liquor magnate, whose shops we have already seen. Weston Square was built by a man called Weston in 1882. To these we will add the Paul Pry Yard, set behind the public house of that name, likewise the setting for a similar group of cottages and workshops.

The Primitive Methodist Chapel

This chapel was built on land adjoining a cottage. It was opened in the autumn of 1872, by the ministers of the Aylsham Primitive Circuit. This was a thriving but poor congregation; the Primitive Methodists belonged largely to the working population of the town, and traditionally were known for their commitment to improving the social and educational prospects of the working classes. Sir George Edwards, who founded the Agricultural Workers Union from his cottage in Sustead Road, Gresham, (see author's *Gresham Voices and Faces*), was a lifelong preacher with the Primitive Methodists. This chapel was in use until the separate strands of Methodism merged in 1932, when it was sold to the Parish Council for £150, and adapted for its new role as Fire Station.

An aerial photo of 1954 helps us establish the layout of this area. There was a narrow roadway entrance between the

PRIMITIVE
METHODIST
CHAPEL
built 1872

chapel and a forge, which led to Chapel Yard. The row of cottages to the right continued virtually to the rear wall of the chapel itself. (The end two of these were demolished to make access for cars, as were the forge and its adjoining cottage on the road.)

A Holt Childhood – Frank Olby

"I was born 3 Chapel Yard, Holt, only one room down; we had a bedroom upstairs and a small box-room; in that house lived my mother, father, my brother, myself, my aunt and my grandmother. My aunt took in washing, my grandmother was an ill person, she had dropsy – so we didn't have a lot of room. At holiday times my aunt used to come from Cromer, with her husband, so when we slept, we sort of like slept in decks. Anyhow, I had a happy childhood there, in Chapel Yard. Gidney, the scrap man at the bottom of the yard, owned all the cottages – I think grandma paid 1/8d a week rent for it. Down the yard on certain days scrap people used to come, there used to be the diddicoys, the gypsies, the travellers bringing their iron and junk, bones and rags round there; and there were horses – there were no motors them days, the horse used to come down, they used to have an old brindle dog running between the axle, of course... There were some characters! They had to knock three of the houses down to make room for the car park.

Further down the yard, the fair used to come on Mr Dick Cooper's land at the very bottom, while the kiddies' amusements were in Chapel Yard itself. This was Gray's Fair, before they went down the Cley road, where Woodrow has his builder's yard. There was the blacksmith's shop, Old Wegg was the blacksmith, and Iky Bullock, who used to do chimney-sweeping. He had a horse and seven... To get his gear in he used to take the driver's seat out, so Iky used to sit on a beer crate, when he went around driving. As for shoeing horses, there was never one that never got shod; if Iky couldn't shoe them standing he used to shoe 'em laying! At that time, Ben Empson used to bring no end of his horses – he had plenty of horses with people going riding, he was a character of Holt. I was horse-mad, I spent all my time round the blacksmith's shop, but the old man would never let you inside the blacksmith's shop. He would put you out, because he was terrified, you know... Those horses, some on 'em were a bit wild!

The Stokes lived up the Cromer Road, where they had Tea Gardens; they had a couple of donkeys, which they used to bring down to be shod. Those donkeys were little devils, so, what Iky do, he used to leave them standing there all day, till the last thing at night, so they got tired of standing, and they were glad to have their shoes put on to go home again!

Mr Hardingham.

Great-grandson John says: "We Hardinghams are one the fittings of Holt!"

Earle Kirby "Charlie Bullock – he was a little fella, I remember in the early days seeing him outside with a blooming great Shire horse, with his apron on, with the hoof between his knees, I used to call as a kid and be fascinated by the forge, watching them bend iron, all that."

Going back to Chapel Yard, there was no water in the house, there was a tap outside shared by six houses; the toilets were down the yard round the corner, so you know what you had to do, if you had one, two in a hurry, and it was night-time an' all... down on the gardens, everybody had a garden. Mr Billy Wright had a shoe shop, where he did shoe repairs, he was a good shoe-repairer an' all – his daughter's still alive today, she lives next to the top fish shop.

The Cockadays of Weston Square

One family who moved into Holt from Norwich in the early years of the twentieth century was the Cockaday family of Weston Square. They made their mark on the life of the town in various areas – and there were plenty of them to do so, as

Cockaday & Sons,
HOLT.

Plumbers, Gas and
Hot Water Fitters
LAWN MOWERS
SUPPLIED & REPAIRED

Any kind of Independent and
Domestic Boiler Supplied and
Fitted.

HOT WATER FITTINGS AND PLUMBING,
TIN AND SHEET IRON WORK.
ELECTRIC BELLS. LOCKSMITHING, Etc.

All kinds of Cooking Ranges
Supplied and Fitted or Repaired.

WORKSHOP WESTON SQUARE.

Archibald (born 1866) and his wife Laura (born 1868) had eleven children. He set up his plumbing business in the Square, operating from this inner courtyard for many years. He also installed his pigeon loft – we see him here with one of his sons, Harry, photographed by a table of trophies glinting in the sun. We have already mentioned the role in town life played by homing pigeons in connection with the Crowe family of Norwich Road, and read of the value to another pigeon-fancier, Gus Clarke, of young Earle Kirby's fleetness of foot. Make a good note of the name Cockaday here, too, as it will recur in the town's story in later decades. Mention should be made as well to the leading role played by Archibald Cockaday, pictured at the head of this chapter in one of the town's Friendly Societies.

rry and Archibald Cockaday

The Paul Pry Inn

This public house has an intriguing name. We have Arthur Hopper to thank for clues to its origin: there is a stage play entitled *Paul Pry* by the dramatist John Poole (1786–1872). This work was put on in Norwich in 1825, where there was also a Paul Pry Inn, whose sign displayed a gentleman in top hat, frock coat and knee-high boots. This figure was also depicted on Holt's sign. By coincidence, an antique collector found a seal featuring a gentleman so attired, with those very words inscribed around the figure. It is assumed that this seal belonged to the actor, a Mr Liston, who took the part in the Norwich theatre. The leading character in the play is a gentleman whose catch phrase is 'I hope I don't intrude'.

I HOPE
I DON'T
INTRUDE

The Paul Pry Yard

Sadly, this yard did not attract the attention of photographers! Living conditions were undoubtedly hard, and it is only in retrospect that they acquire a certain patina of charm. As a child, Doreen Abrams visited the workshops of Knowles the tailors, which were situated here.

Reg Crowe, seen here outside the Paul Pry, was working as baker's boy for Messrs WA Newell at Hempstead Mill in 1917.

Doreen Abrams "There were tiny cottages there, I was small, but I can remember, they had a pump in yard for water, and two privies in the centre of the yard, and the old ladies used to sit in the cottage windows, with a canary, or a lamp."

However, one key photograph has recently emerged This shows the Knowles tailors seated, as they used to be, for their work.

Edith Pointin's brother, Bob White, worked there all his life.

Edith Pointin "My brother Robert, or Bobbie as they called him, worked as fitter and cutter for 55 years. Mr Knowles supplied all the Gresham's School boys with clothes. They were all made up at the tailor's shop by about seven men who always sat on the hard floor to sew."

Eva Lord "The same men were always there – we used to have clothes made there, overcoats and things. Bob White used to measure you, they were first-class things – but they lasted a bit too long for young people, who wanted a change!" *(Laughter.)*

Lees Yard

This long brick structure, originally a warehouse for Alfred Lee, bears the date stamp 1896. We have already seen the two Lee shops, one on the corner where New Street joins the High Street, and the other further towards the Market Place, on the north side. The construction of this warehouse must have seemed outlandish at the time, in terms of both scale and colour of brick. The railway had been opened just twelve years earlier, and this new means of transport brought an entrepreneur like Alfred Lee the opportunity to depart from traditional flint and red brick.

Clearly, his was a thriving business, and here he stands, proudly presenting his workforce, his distribution team and his newly-built premises. It all represents a substantial investment. Alfred Lee's grandson Neville has provided the following information about the building.

Neville Lee "Most of the upper storey, extending as far as the open doorway, where the man is standing with a bale of hay, was probably a beer store. The hoist we can see in operation was active throughout the first part of the century, at least until the 1940s. To the right of the open double doors were stables, which were, however, later converted to use as a storage area for wholesale groceries.

Alfred Lee and his wife Amelia May Lee

Stables were then built on the eastern end of Lees Yard, and these were in use until the late 1930s. The brickwork holds stone plaques at intervals, each with an engraving of initials.

AL 1896 – Alfred Lee
AML 1896 – Amelia May Lee, his wife
WCL 1896 – William Cooper Lee
(brother of Alfred?)
RFB 1896 – (unknown)
NRL 1999 – Nick Lyle (who converted the building into residential/retail/office accommodation)"

Shirehall Plain

As for every area of the town, our information is useful but incomplete. We will consider each key building in turn, looking at their varied use in different decades. We'll start with the most prominent of all, the brick water tower, built in 1885 and demolished in the mid-1950s.

The Water Tower

The tower's chosen location might not have been the most convenient in terms of the way life developed in the twentieth century, but its position here in Shirehall Plain certainly ensured its central role in the early years. It is interesting to speculate whether it would have avoided demolition if it had been somewhere that did not prove a nuisance to motor vehicles. It was taken down (and the base blown up, such was its solidity) in the mid-fifties, that decade that had little time for, and even less sensitivity to, the splendours of Victorian engineering. Many photos survive of this structure, but none shows its brickwork to better effect than this. The stepped base, the play with depth on its sides, the crenellated detail: this was a fine, solid structure, but never leaden. Like its partner, the Pump House on the Spout Hills, it was a lovely blend of function and grace.

Enough of the beauty, now the work! The tower was 56 ft high, and its tank held 15,000 gallons, pumped from the Hills, piped through the town and on up to the top. The man who oversaw this operation was Arnold Burrell, Waterworks Manager, and his role earned him a place on the Parish Council. A balance had to be struck at all times between rate of supply and consumption, and it was his job to maintain it. Eva Lord, whose home above the shop (FW Baker, see page 100) gave directly onto the tower, made this observation:

Eva Lord "The water was pumped up from the Spout Hills to the water tower; occasionally it used to run over, and Mr Burrell, who was brother to the two school mistresses, used to have to come and turn the water off; but sometimes he didn't come at once, and all the water was coming up and being wasted, so the little boys used to go across and tell him. In the Burrell's house, there was a big plate with pennies on, and the boys used to get a penny for telling him the water ran over."

Edith Pointin adds a personal dimension.

Edith Pointin "When the tower was full, the water gushed out of a pipe into a drain. We children would run to Mr Burrell's house and then on home, because he would always give us a penny. But I sometimes got told off by Daddy, as he worked for Mr Burrell, who'd say to me, 'Go and ask your father to stop the engines!' This meant a walk over the Hills. However, I was pleased, because sometimes he'd let me go with him to watch the engines."

The outside of the tower looked fine, but what of the inside? John Jarvis and John Turner both remember it, and this description has been compiled from their recollections.

Step inside the double doors, and you were in a tall empty space, with a wooden staircase that zigzagged up to the platform which supported the tank. From there, a steel ladder bolted to the wall could provide access to the roof, if you were prepared to squeeze through a small gap between the circular tank and the wall. A trapdoor was now the only obstacle between you and the sky, and if you opened it, poked your head out and looked around on the lead roof, you saw... tennis balls. Lobbing them to the top of the tower was clearly a popular pursuit among certain of Holt's population!

The water level in the tank could be read from the ground. Marks were painted on the wall, and a metal weight, suspended by cords attached to a float in the tank, gave a reading to the practised eye. The only other items to be seen were the canvas hoses of the Fire Service hanging from pulleys at the base of the platform. Which brings us to – the Holt's Fire Service.

‎ra Hills "Then there was ‎nold Burrell – he was ‎anager of the water works ‎d didn't we know it! – he'd ‎me after us if we let the ‎s run, see a little water ‎ibbling from an outside ‎o, he'd be there. 'Turn that ‎o off, you're wasting ‎ater.'"

‎rle Kirby "I belonged to ‎e New Street gang, as kids. ‎was funny, because we ‎ed to get up to all sorts, ‎e Peacock Lane gang, the ‎ck Street gang, the ‎mpstead Road gang, the ‎rwich Road gang... The ‎w Street gang held ‎mmand, if I can put it like ‎at, of the Hills. But ‎mehow we'd end up by ‎ving a fight at the bottom ‎the water tower, which ‎as the focal point of our ‎tivities."

The Fire Service

In the first part of the century, the Fire Station was an old brick building between the Methodist Chapel and cottages on that side of Norwich Road. It then moved to the rear of the Shirehall – that part which now accommodates Nationwide. Later on, it was housed in the former Primitive Methodist Chapel. Sited in the Shirehall Plain, the adjacent water tower proved very convenient from more than one point of view; it provided the water, yes, but also the perfect internal space to hang the hoses. On return from an operation, it was necessary to hoist up the canvas hoses, hose them down – then hang them to dry.

One particular blaze lives on.

Byfords – Fire!

The first fire in Holt – the eighteenth century one, the fire that razed most of Holt to the ground – had almost as disastrous a sequel nearly two hundred years later. That time it broke out very close to the centre of Holt and its key buildings. The same was true for the more recent occasion too – except that the hub of the town had moved in the meantime. Early on Sunday morning, November 18th 1906, smoke was detected, the alarm raised, and neighbours were on the scene. Mrs Beresford was soon followed by Mr CW Jex, who quickly summoned the Fire Brigade. Fortunately, as we now appreciate, the brigade was stationed rather conveniently, as was a plentiful supply of water, but everybody was aware of a major fear: the shop stored quantities of both gunpowder and cartridges, and the flames were fierce. Nearby houses were evacuated, Mr Crowe's stables emptied, and the firemen were desperately trying to maintain an adequate flow of water. They were quickly joined by a reserve force of 'several members of the Parish Council, who were early in evidence and rendered yeoman service.' Together they fought to prevent the fire spreading to other properties. Then the gunpowder exploded – but 'it was wonderful that nobody was injured.' However, 'B Matthews, an auxiliary fireman, had his eyebrows singed and his cap carried high in the air by the explosion which made a large hole in a 14-inch wall.' The blaze did not reach the cartridges, however. The destruction to the rear of the property was so great, and the heat so intense, that firemen had to remain on watch the following day.

Afterwards came the opportunity for recognition of the concerted effort made by so many, and by the Waterworks Manager in particular, 'for the dexterity he displayed in setting the hose attached to the hydrants and for the plentiful supply of water at the disposal of the brigade throughout.' (Norfolk News, 24th November 1906).

Sixty years on, Holt having enjoyed considerable advances in technology in the meantime, John King looks back with a slightly superior gaze to a very early fire engine prototype:

One amusing small-town episode lives vividly in the memory. Holt had an old-fashioned archaic fire-engine, a sort of Heath Robinson construction, which was even more primitive on occasions by its motive power. It was a four-wheeled vehicle consisting of a tank with long bars on either side for pumping, manned on each side by three or four men. The action of pumping drew water into the tank and then pumped it onto the fire. Though this machine could be drawn by a horse, it was not uncommon for it to be manhandled by the pumping team, who galloped along with the vehicle with themselves as the motive power. This was a funny sight in itself – fat, hot, sweaty men, their feet champing up and down as they went to a fire or to a practice on the Spout Hills, passing that famous landmark, Blind Sam, a drinking-fountain-cum-sign-and-lamp-post, which used to stand in the centre of the town outside the Old School House of Gresham's School, but which was moved to the top of Letheringsett Hill when the War Memorial took its place.

On this occasion there was a house on fire not far from Salthouse Heath, and very close to the old aerodrome at Bayfield Brecks. This was 2½ miles away, down steepish hills, and no doubt a horse was procured to pull the machine there and back. Alas! It took time to collect the crew and to arrive at the scene of the fire; and once there, in their hurry, the firemen assembled their apparatus wrongly and the water already in the tank was pumped back into the conveniently-sited pond. And by the time it was properly re-assembled and ready to function, it was too late! The house had been destroyed and the fire burnt out.

Great was the consternation of the firemen and great the amusement of the town when they got to hear of the mishap! With scorn and derision, the firemen became a laughing-stock. Indeed, their chagrin at the happening was so bitter that they threatened to resign as a body and leave Holt without a fire-fighting crew. This was a serious threat and it was taken seriously. Their wrath was only mollified, eventually appeased and their wounded vanity healed when they were treated to a dinner by the public to mark its appreciation of their devoted and painstaking service.

is was the dinner in estion.

It Almanack, May 3rd 1928.

show appreciation of the rk of the Holt Fire Brigade, subscription dinner, ganised by Messrs JJ llows, JW Fox and FA well, was held at the White n Hotel, when a company mbering over forty spent a st enjoyable time. Mr F rtley presided, supported Mr TA Cook, the Revd AH cher, and members of the rish Council.

Ethel Potter "The Byford family ironmongers, where there is now a smart restaurant, were a big help when we were young. Mrs Byford and her daughters would help if we were doing plays; she would take us through our lines. They had a son Ron who would sing a song about buying a watch from Woolworths Bazaar and his rendering of the Farmer's Boy would have us all in tears."

The Byford family

There's no mention of the family in Kelly's Directory of 1896, but in 1900 we read 'Byford Henry, furnishing & general ironmonger, tinman, locksmith & general repairer'. The business soon became well-established and central to the life of the town and district. The Byford's delivery cart made a regular tour of surrounding villages.

There were four children born to Henry and his wife, two boys, Clifford and Ronnie, and two girls, Cassie and Queenie. Neither Ronnie nor Queenie married, but they were both very active in town life; Ronnie was a musician and scoutmaster, while Queenie worked for the Red Cross.

The Shirehall

This building is a predominantly eighteenth century structure, on one of the oldest built sites in the town. Until its sale into private ownership in the seventies, it had been the core of the town's administration. It was both law court and council chamber. It was used, too, for political meetings and social gatherings. When the Holt bench of magistrates was absorbed into a different regional arrangement in 1975, the court closed for ever. The last Clerk, TD Savory, wrote a short history in honour of its work over preceding centuries. He gives the following account of its early history as a building.

> The Shirehall at Holt is one of the few ancient buildings of that town, which used to be called Holt Market. In mediaeval times it was the corn market house where tolls were collected and fines were imposed for breach of standard weights and measures. This was long before shops as we know them were invented in England. The original size of the tollhouse was 46ft by 25ft. In course of time it became the meeting place of the Justices sitting in Quarter and Petty Sessions, as at Little Walsingham, and for general purposes.

He goes on to outline practices early in the twentieth century, and to record the names of some of those involved.

> It may be that magistrates came into Holt on Market Day, looking in at the Court House to see whether they were needed to sit. The clerk has found this very useful on many occasions when requiring a Juvenile bench at short notice or on occasions such as the prosecution many years ago of Major Philip Hamond, a member of the Holt Bench for assaulting the Reverend Harold Davidson of Stiffkey. Between 1910 and 1942 Mr Temple Lynes of Blakeney, Mr Arthur Cozens-Hardy of Cley, Colonel Watson-Kennedy of Wiveton and Mr Walter

CW Jex stands with his
[wif]e at the door to the first
[of] his many enterprises in
[the] town. Not just a butcher,
[oh] no, but an English and
[Co]lonial Meat and Game
[Pu]rveyor. This photo was
[tak]en early in the century.
[Yo]u may recall his heroics in
[the] Byfords blaze; and we
[ha]ve also discovered that, in
[the] First World War, he took
[the] lease of the building we
[no]w call Oddfellows Hall,
[ch]ristening it Town Hall in
[the] process. There he put on
[va]rious entertainments,
[wh]ose titles included the
[gr]acious *The Earls and the
[Gir]ls* and *The Maids and the
[Ad]dies*. (NB I had to look up
['ad]diy', too!) His is a name
[to] watch.

Towler of Edgefield were respectively Chairmen, but there may have been others. Miss Kate Brereton of Briningham was appointed a JP in the early 1920s, being one of the first lady magistrates in the country to go on the Bench. Some of the cases are more interesting than others. On one occasion, a particular gamekeeper, Old Harry, had caught a notorious poacher red-handed. Now Harry in the witness box was always good value and very popular with the public gallery. Needless to say, most of the gamekeepers in the neighbourhood managed to find a reason to be in Holt that morning and look in at the court. On another occasion, there was a dispute concerning a married couple who, following a swarm of their bees, were assaulted by their neighbours. A great battle between the 'Hittites' and the 'Hivites' took place – and was fought again, in words, in court.

The red-brick building attached to the rear of the Shirehall, now two cottages (one of them Street Davies, estate agent), was formerly the manse, occupied by the minister to the United Reform Church. Before then, it had been a public house, owned by the Cozens-Hardy family. The Crowe general store on the corner of the lane to Lees Yard was the gas showroom, where Gus Holt, lamp-lighter, was based.

The Parish Council

This body took over the administration of town affairs from the church-based Vestry Meeting in 1894. Thereafter, it sat in the Shirehall. A swift perusal of the Minutes lodged at the Norfolk Record Office reveals the following ongoing concerns: Fire Brigade, Street Lighting, Street Watering, the Waterworks, Sports, Burials. There was also some resentment in the early years about how the changed status of Gresham's would affect the availability of local scholarships. (See Chapters 7 & 8.) Some felt that the town had 'lost' its own school. Here is a brief report from the 1929 Holt Almanack.

The triennial Parish meeting for the election of a Parish Council was held in the Shirehall, Mr TM Larner being elected to the chair. The voting was done by a show of hands, and those elected were: FR Bailey, 102; HW Moulton, 86; H Bond and Mrs Field, 79; RJ Chapman, 78; CW Jex, 77; JC Miller, 75; F Starling, FS Minns, 71; WJ Elsden, 64; Mrs Reid, 62; CE Winn, 55; M Abbs, 45. Not elected: J Bramley, W Knights, 43 and F Duggen, 9. Mr HW Moulton asked the meeting to

View up Tower Street, showing the reason for its name. Note the date 1744 on the side wall of Hanworth House.

express their appreciation of the many years service given to the Council by their late Chairman, Mr SL Gooch. Mr Gooch had been on the Council since its formation in 1894.

Bull Street (formerly Tower Street)

In early postcards this street is always referred to as Tower Street as it used to lead to the water tower.

A Holt Childhood – Betty Mann

"I was born in Bull Street. The house is a posh shop now, called Deborah's, right on the corner with the alleys. My mother and father were both Holt people; at first my father had a shop but after he came back from the war he went to Byfords. They were nice people, we could walk in when we liked, they did Brownies and Guides, they helped you get ready for concerts. Our mother had five children, four girls, and one boy, but he died, he had a twisted bowel; Dr Hales was the doctor. I went to the Board School down New Street. We had oil-lamps at home, and dry toilets.

We had lovely Christmasses – we didn't have marvellous presents like they do today – you were lucky if you got an apple, orange, a few sweets. Our biggest treat was coming into town on Christmas Eve with my mum and dad, when we went to our grandma's house; Eva Baker's shop was all lit up, with her doll's house. Our childhood games consisted of playing tops and skips and hoops, we did that in the street, there was no traffic. The International Stores was where Alliance & Leicester now is, and my aunt worked there. There was a garage called Robinson's where they showed silent films, and a Miss Cook used to play the piano, the rain used to patter on the roof. She had an office, right in the pathway, where she took the money. My cousin and I were never separated as kids, we played duets together, I'd spend my weekends with her. We went to Sunday School three times a day. Mum and Dad used to meet us in the afternoon and we used to walk miles after that. Then we had our tea before the service at night. I used to love to go for a walk on a Sunday afternoon so I could hold my father's arm.

My Grandma had the first telephone in Holt, the shop down the Back Street, next to Osocozi. It was a little thing, in the backroom. My father once phoned from France. Later on, a friend and I used to man the telephone exchange to let them have a night out, on the Saturday night, that was a lovely night of the week that was, 'cos young men used to phone us up, they knew we were on duty! As children, we spent all the day on the Spout Hills; we used to go round the Lowes, too, that was a lovely walk down there; and Selbrigg, we went there. On Armistice Day, as a child, I thought all the soldiers were buried in the War Memorial! Thinking of that, I can remember Blind Sam being taken down the other end; the horses used to drink out of that."

WATER TOWER

built 1885
demolished 1950s

Between school and marriage

"After I left school on the Friday, I started a five-year's apprenticeship on the Monday. I was apprenticed in dressmaking to Madame Helene in Sheringham; I went by train – I missed the train on the first morning, so I arrived late. There were four or five girls under me by the time I left. We worked mostly with jersey, made one suit a day, with pockets; we'd start off with the skirt and get so far. That became a regular thing, you had to get so much done by a certain stage in the day. You did it because you loved it. The workshops were down by the Lobster, right opposite there. The thing was, we had to be there by nine, and if we went by train, it didn't arrive till twenty past. So we used to cycle, several of us together; first Mary Beresford, she was the first one I'd pick up, then we'd go to Crossways at High Kelling, where there'd be Mrs Rawling's husband Jack, then on to Bodham, where we'd pick the twins up, go a little further and pick another man up... so, we all went sailing off together! I did it for five years, then the doctor advised me to give it up, I was working too hard. I worked on my own then, until I got married at the age of twenty-two. Mum was ever so strict. You thank her for it. Mum was a nanny when she was young, we had to behave ourselves. My future husband and I went out for about two years before we got married, and I honestly and truly think my mum wouldn't leave us alone in the house until it was my marriage time, she was that strict."

Hanworth House

This is a very characteristic piece by Jane Hales, evoking a habitat peopled by characters we would barely recognise now, hidden behind that mat of ivy. In the early years of the twentieth century, Hanworth House was a boarding-house run by two sisters, the Misses West. We know that Vivian Smith, Art Master at Gresham's, lived here, as did Mr Mould, Head Master of the Church School after Matt Pearson.

Clad in ivy, Hanworth House is barely visible through the foliage. Today you might recognise it as the premises of Larking Gowen accountants.

It is a tall house, built in 1744, standing beside the narrow Bull Street. The upper windows overlook a jumble of tiled cottages, And beyond them the open space of Fish Hill and the inn with the chestnut tree beside it. When the Misses West first came to the tall house in the late nineteenth century, they were a little apprehensive about the ghost and how it would affect the lodgers, not to mention the maidservant. It was quite a common variety of ghost – a lady in a silk dress, who descended by a steep back staircase from a room on the upper storey. The Misses West partitioned the room, and all the time they were in the tall house they were never troubled by any supernatural lady.

The tall house, with its many windowed eyes, was defiant, its high pitched gables withstood the bitter winds from the Pole, tearing across the dark heaths on the shuddering Market Town. And when spring came, and the April Fair Day, it had looked out into clear sunshine, on to the people from the villages, who had thronged thither to buy and sell, and let themselves for the ensuing year, as manservant or maidservant.

Employees of William Royall doing work on a cottage in Tower Street: Herbert Green is on the ladder, with Barney MacMahon below. Looking ahead, we see the White Lion, with the brick chimney to its brewery just visible.

When the Misses West first came to the tall house, they engaged a strong girl, called Rebecca, as a maidservant, who declared that she was 'clevered to work'. So she proved to be, for Rebecca stayed at the tall house for ten years, till she was married and had a family. Thereafter she sent a Christmas card to the Misses West, conveyed by some of her children, whose spokesmen said 'they were ter wait for an answer'.

The rooms at the tall house were always full, and small wonder for the Misses West looked after their lodgers as a family. They mended for the bachelors; their cooking could not be bettered. The joys and troubles of their lodgers were as their own. No-one who stayed at the tall house was ever forgotten. If one of them died in some far away part of the world, the younger Miss West wept at the chimney corner. As to bills, the Misses West did make them out to be sure, but their charges did not mount with the times. 'Well you see,' they would explain, 'we charged him that when he stayed here twenty years ago, and we couldn't make an alteration now.'

Most of the business of the tall house was conducted in the kitchen, a low room, with ham hooks in the ceiling, and a floor of square bricks, uneven with age. Here, at any hour of the day and into the night, might be found the Misses West at work, and apparently undisturbed by many visitors. For not only did the lodgers congregate in this warm place, but people from the town outside. If somebody hungered for gossip, the most likely place to find satisfaction was in that kitchen. Though the sisters seldom moved far from the house, the colourful life from outside came into it – young men with high hopes, old women with sad stories.

The scullery opened out of the kitchen, and here between the copper and the boiler, sat Alfred, drooping, asthmatical, and extremely untidy, eating up the scraps, and feeding on uncounted plates of porridge. He was one of those people who, in the Norfolk term, 'Never git no further than Tuesday'. He had left a job many years before to look after his sick mother, though he had no means of supporting her. Now he worked, or rather pottered about, for the Misses West, to whom he was passionately attached. Sometimes ignorant lodgers gave Alfred tips, which he immediately converted into drinks, to his more pronounced derangement. Picture postcards gave him great pleasure; he would show his birthday collection to anyone who would look at them. 'That there came away from So-and-So' he would say. It was a bad day for Alfred when the younger Miss West was taken to hospital by ambulance. Alfred was prying round the corner to see her go. Afterwards he was found disconsolate in the scullery. 'I see'd them take har away' he sobbed, 'and she didn't niver give one kick'.

A Holt Childhood – Dorothy High

"My parents were not Holt people, they were from London, and I came to Holt when I was four; I was born in 1918. They were my adoptive parents – and I was the only one. I was lonely at times, but I had a very good father and mother. We first lived at the end of the alleys, where the NFU now is. It was a wet fish shop, and then we did fish and chips – on Saturdays they never closed until eleven o'clock. Dad made the ice-cream down in the cellar, too; Mum had a flag hanging out of the window. We often played with hoops up and down the alleys. We were there until I was about eleven years old, when we moved to Shirehall Plain. We were near Byfords, and the Post Office was in between us and Byfords – now Dees. When we were a bit older, we had dances up the Drill Hall, we had Keep Fit in the Church Hall; once we went to Felbrigg Hall, we did dancing on the lawn there, with Ketton Cremer. Then when I was a bit older we went roller-skating in Cromer. When I left school at fourteen I worked for a year in the Egg place down New Street – the old Board School premises – for about a year. Then I worked in Sheringham for three years – we biked there every day, had to be there for half past eight, didn't leave on Fridays until after seven o'clock. Now that's a long way to bike. If it was a rainy day we were allowed to go on the train. I wasn't very big and I wasn't very strong, I was about sixteen or seventeen… "

detail from brickwork of Bakers shop
ironmongers since 1782

FISH
HILL

LIVESTOCK
MARKET

closed
1960

SPOT

FEATHERS
HOTEL

CHAPTER
FIVE

BLIND SAM

THE
QUEEN VICTORIA
JUBILEE
LANTERN

Chapter 5

FW Baker proudly announces his store from the rooftops. We can just see the Reliance Printing Works of Arthur Preston, far left.

A Holt Childhood – Eva Lord

Eva is the daughter of FW Baker, who ran a department store of that name on the corner of High Street and Shirehall Plain. Here she talks of her home.

Eva Lord (née Baker) "We lived in the building that's now occupied by Abbotts the house agents. My father's shop comprised drapery, boots and shoes, carpets and we lived above the shop in a very large flat. The dining-room faced the water tower which has since been demolished where we had wonderful Christmas parties. Our sitting-room, or drawing-room as it was then called, faced the Feathers Hotel, where we used to watch the Friday market. My mother's father ran the shop, and then my father, who worked at a wholesale house in London, took it over when his father-in-law died. And then my brother took it over when our father died, in the early part of the Second World War. There were three cottages attached to our shop, and they belonged to my mother; and the old people paid five shillings a week, and they got a pound of tea at Christmas. But they were quite satisfied and happy. We didn't have a garden – we spent all our playtime on Saturdays on the Spout Hills, they had horses feeding on the Hills. There was an old boy who gave them a wide berth, he used to sleep there all the summer... his name was Tory Abram – in the wintertime they gave him a shed at the gasworks. The rector at the time was the Revd HA King, who had nine children, they had this marvellous garden down Letheringsett Hill. From the time we were about seven, the girls all joined the Brownies, and later the Guides, and we used to go down to the Rectory, and have the most marvellous time down there. We'd paddle in the stream; he was a wonderful man. They were paid very badly at that time, and every

Sunday morning, would walk up to the church to take the service, with about five of the children side by side – I can see them now. Then, as time went on, he had a motor-bike, and he had his cassock underneath and he used to have it flowing out either side, I can see it now going down the street. There he comes! (Laughter.) Do I digress?

When Mrs King had the last little girl, somebody said: 'Poor Mrs King, what, another baby?' Her husband was heard to reply, 'My wife takes those things as a woman should.' That soon shut them up! (Laughter, followed by more laughter.) Mrs King was a very nice lady, she was captain of the Guides. She had something to do with the Girls' Friendly Society, which was connected with the Guides, and she used to have us down there for tea."

Eva tells us of her early schooling, which was in a very convenient location.

ne Hales Elden House In e house now occupied by oyds Bank, was the shop of r Burrell, the basket-maker. e grew osiers in a field by e Grove Lane, and had out thirty women to strip em in season, and his was familiar figure until well to the present century.

"The first school I went to was in Elden House, exactly opposite our shop, the house where Lloyds Bank is now. Mostly the farmers' daughters went there.

The school was run by two maiden ladies, Edith and Hilda Burrell, and of course they seemed quite old to us at the time, but they must have been late thirties or early forties. We were not allowed any playtime, we went from nine till twelve, and they charged four guineas a term. All the tradesmen's children went there, and in the very early days, my father, who had the shop opposite, used to come and fetch me and bring me back – but it was just the other side of the road; we had only about two cars in Holt then, but even so he always used to come for me. They used to be most annoyed if he came before twelve o'clock. When the Armistice was signed, Edith Burrell came in the room and said, 'The Armistice has been signed; you can all go home!' Great glee, so we had the rest of the day off. Of course the Memorial was not built at that time of day, the Jubilee Lantern stood there in its place. It was removed to the other end of the town, when the Memorial was erected. Everybody thought it was a great expense, because it cost £400. They had the peace celebrations there about six months later, because peace wasn't signed until six months after the end of the fighting. That's when they had parties in the town."

Eva spent her working life in the Post Office, so she took particular note of the changes in its location.

"I first remember the Post Office in Clare's, in the Market Place, a bookshop one side, the Post Office the other. Then during the war they had to move, and they couldn't get anywhere, so my father let half his shop to the Post Office. There was a partition put up – drapery one side, the Post Office the other – and they had the use of our back yard for their vehicles and things. They had two telegraph girls who used to deliver telegrams. It was there for over two years. Then it moved next door to Byfords."

Eva completed her schooling in Norwich.

"Later, I went away to school in Norwich – Lonsdale House, Earlham Road when I was twelve and a half; there were several girls from Holt; two maiden ladies kept the school, they were very strict and very religious. I was there four years – lots of the time was happy, and some of it was not." (Laughter.)

The time came to leave.

"I was sixteen, my father came up to the school and said, my daughter is leaving tomorrow, she's got the chance of learning the Post Office, and I had to start my training the next day. I was pleased, I'd had enough of boarding school, it's not all honey. I had six months training, because it was all Morse Code on these sounders, you know, sending telegrams. But I had a good start, because I'd learnt Morse Code in the Guides. There was a vacancy in Holt, so I was able to live at home. The first time I got my full pay of £2, I went down to Ransom's and bought a new pair of shoes, brogues."

She moves on to other memories.

"Then there was an old boy who used to catch rabbits called Tenth Nurse, and he used to walk miles and miles and miles – Roly Nurse in Holt would be his great-grandson. Some of these old boys – there was another old boy called Dalby – they all used to congregate outside our shop – at one time they called that 'Poverty Corner'!

A close look behind the men on the right shows the location of the Post Office.

They used to go round picking up cigarette ends, you know... Every Saturday evening the Salvation Army played outside our shop. There was a Scottish man, Mr McCormack, who lived in Holt at the time, he used to play the concertina most wonderfully – they're difficult instruments to play, you know. And of course we would have our windows open at the top, the three bedrooms along the top, and it was quite an event every Saturday night; we had to throw a coin, it used to be a penny; they sang all the hymns – they had a marvellous band."

Her near-neighbour was Gooch, the chemist.

"My mother always said to me, 'Go and ask Mr Gooch what he recommends.' They didn't have doctors until it was really necessary, you know, so Stephen Gooch had to recommend some sort of – well you didn't have pills then, he'd mix up something, you know, like coloured water! (laughter) Then there was the other chemist in town, Bernard Craske and his father, who they used to call Tibby. My mother wouldn't take pills. So Mr Craske got some jellied sweets, cut them in the middle, put the pill there, then seal them up again. Then I'd give her the jellied sweets and she'd take the pill. They were up to all sorts of tricks in those days."

Eva has particularly strong memories of The Feathers Hotel.

e Feathers Hotel, 1924
e decoration was the
ndiwork of Arthur
rgess, sign-writer.

a Lord All the tradesmen
ent to the Feathers
cause they liked the lady
hind the bar! She was a
ry capable lady. She
ways had somebody to
ok after the children.

"I remember when Mr Cubitt Cooke first came to Holt. He was married to a young woman, he was in his late fifties, and he was married to a young woman of twenty-four – a lovely-looking lady she was – and very popular running the hotel. And they had three daughters, and I remember them being born. I was about eight or nine at the time. Cubitt Cooke had the front of the hotel all painted in lurid colours, lovely pinks and blues – Holt being rather an old-fashioned place, it was a bit startling at first! But they were a very nice family. Once a week, he came out with his gig – quite a high gig – dressed in a very smart way, jacket and top hat. He used to ride with one of his horses – a racing horse – up and down the town – it was quite a spectacle once a week. I think he owned a racing stable at Newmarket. They used to come across to the shop, because my father made a lot of fuss of children. Mr Knowles and his wife, who didn't have children, were particularly fond of the dark one, they practically adopted her; she used to sit on the counter while Mr Knowles was cutting out the suits. They were such friendly little children.

They had a bowling-green at the end of the Feathers Yard; all the tradesmen played bowls, my dad included. They had matches periodically, when they'd go out and play against the villages, and they'd win. But they all had a prize (laughter), like a glass bowl or jug or something like that, so they were very happy!"

The Feathers Hotel and the Cubitt Cooke family

Mother and three daughters, Pauline, Mary and Doreen.

Between the years 1918–27 the landlord of The Feathers Hotel was Mr C Cubitt Cooke, who lived there with his wife and three daughters, Pauline, Mary, and Doreen. Pauline was already with her parents when the family came to Holt; the other two, Mary and Doreen, were born in the town, delivered, so they were always told, by Dr Hales. I had the good fortune to sit in on a conversation between the three of them on their annual return to Norfolk in June.

Doreen Abrahams (née Cubitt Cooke) "My father's story goes like this… his own father thrashed him, so he ran away to London on a cattle-truck; he went to stay at the Wig and Pen, which is opposite the Law Courts, with his uncle, who sent him to St Clement Dane's school. Another uncle saw his potential and introduced him to the hotel trade. As a young man, there's the story of him taking his horse into the Café Royal as a bet. He was challenged, to which he replied: 'If that horse goes, I go, too' – so the horse stayed!"

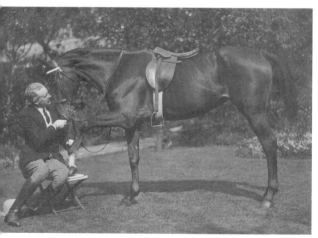

Cubitt Cooke. Man and horse – a love affair.

Pauline Cubitt "He rode the horse into the Café Royal, up the staircase, along the balcony, and down the other side, for a wager. He was a very handsome man."

Mary Whitmore (née Cubitt Cooke) "His great friend was old Walter Gilbey (of the gin family) – they were two of a kind!"

Mr Cubitt Cooke is entertaining to hear about – but what kind of man was he?

Pauline "I suppose he was entertaining to people in the Feathers, he had many friends, I know."

Mary "Well, shall we say, er, drinkers?"

Pauline "Not only that…"

Mary "One of his great friends was Matt Pearson, who became Town Clerk."

Pauline "Mr Pearson became our guardian, he was very kind to us."

They talk about life in the town.

This is the Feathers Bowling Green. Budgens store now occupies this site.

Pauline "Our father was owner of hotel, cattle-yard, bowling-green, the flower garden and a field, he had his horses grazing there. We had a stable. Father had about four horses; he had a dear old sow called Daisy, she was very vicious, and she had some piglets. He also had a lovely sheepdog called Joe, who was very naughty. Now this dog Joe had a taste for people on bicycles, he got the old Rector of Stiffkey off his bicycle – the famous Rector of Stiffkey, Harold Davidson, he used to come to Holt on market day and speak to everybody, but Joe would pull him off his bicycle."

Mary "But Joe would mainly go for motorcycles – he was an expert at it – after the war, you know, all these village boys loved these motorcycles, and they would dash through the town and that was a red rag to a bull to Joe."

Animals feature prominently in their memories, and animals were central to the role of the Feathers in those years, as the Friday livestock market took place in the yard behind the hotel. Drovers brought animals from neighbouring farms into Holt, while cattle from further afield arrived by train and then were herded through the town.

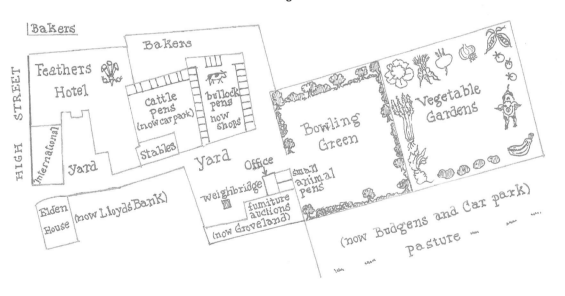

The map above shows just how much land was owned by the Feathers; this included the market area immediately behind the hotel, with bowling-green, gardens, a 'lovely summerhouse where the men used to sit', and pasture beyond.

Doreen "You can still see where the bulls used to be tethered, the rings there, in the old market yard. And the tiles, too – Mother said if the man didn't turn up to clean between the tiles on market day, they would have lost the licence, so she had to clean them and they were little, tiny tiles."

Pauline "I remember as a little girl, climbing up on this wall, going along, and there was one cow left after the market. I did not realize he was a bull. So I decided to let the poor creature out. I climbed over and down, pulled up the peg – and out shot the bull! It went down the High Street and into a builders' yard. And whenever I did anything wrong, I went to Daddy, and he said, 'What have you done wrong?' He jolly well knew I'd done something wrong, I was awful."

Mary "They used to take the bulls round at the back, where there was a butcher's and stun them there."

Doreen "We had an ostler, and rats!"

Cubitt Cooke never took to the motor car, but prided himself on a small yellow Victorian coach which would meet guests at the railway station.

Mary "At that time the hotel guests were not holiday-makers. A lot of commercial travellers stayed, as did many parents from Gresham's School – half-term used to be very busy. There were about twelve bedrooms, no coffee bar, or anything like that, that's where the stables were."

High Street Neighbours

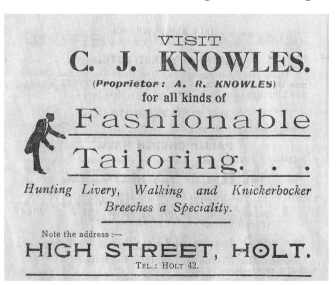

VISIT
C. J. KNOWLES.
(Proprietor: A. R. KNOWLES)
for all kinds of
Fashionable
Tailoring. . .
Hunting Livery, Walking and Knickerbocker Breeches a Speciality.

Note the address :—
HIGH STREET, HOLT.
Tel.: Holt 42.

Together, they recall their neighbours in the High Street.

Mary "Knowles the tailors were opposite us, they seemed to be under contract to do the gamekeepers' suits for all the big estates, I used to go along with my uncle to measure them up."

Doreen "He used to employ disabled people from the First World War, perhaps men with one leg, and they were wielding these enormous irons, pressing away… Another thing, three car-loads of the Knowles family and our family used to go cockling on Stiffkey marshes, and the Broads, too."

Mary "Oh, I must tell you a lovely tale about the Knowles. On a Sunday – they had a Wyvern, Vauxhall, car, you know, with a hood that came down, and Mrs Knowles was learning to drive, and she was about 70-odd, and I was stuck in the middle, and Fred used to put his arm over and touch her on the arm, and she was only doing twenty or so, and he'd say, 'Steady, woman!' It was gorgeous, it really was."

Next to Knowles was Gooch the chemist.

Pauline "Mr Gooch the chemist used to prepare all the little medicines or tablets for the farmers to collect on Fridays, and there was a little conservatory with a box outside where the medicines were put – until he had a break-in, he was very upset about this, so he put a tree in the conservatory plus a snake – Do Not Touch! But I think everything went all right. He used to chase us children, if we got in the alleyway, because we all went to look for the snake!"

phen Gooch, Walter
stney and a lady
nding in the shop
rway.

Doreen "Miss Hall kept the sweetshop, at the corner of the drive."

Pauline "On the other side of the road, there was a fruit shop, kept by Mrs Waller, who was a dear old lady; she always served customers with a hat on. If we were very good, we got some cherries."

Another memory stirs.

Pauline "I was about seven, I think, my fingers had warts all over them. I cried at these things coming on my fingers, I don't know how they got there, they were nasty. Nanny took us to this charmer, Mrs Bird; what did she do? She put meat on my fingers – and buried it. The warts went."

Mary "She lived in a little cottage up the Norwich Road, near Dr Hales, because we waited outside while you went in."

While at the other end of town...

Mary "Mrs Pope lived at the bottom of the town in a most beautiful Georgian house, where she kept about thirty small dogs, really small ones; and when she used to walk about the town, they were on leads. She had a son who was at Eton; now her husband died, and when the poor lad came home for his holidays, she used to sit up there in the cemetery with him for ages, all dressed in black, it was really pathetic. And this makes me think of the funerals, with the plumed horses, and the blinds all pulled down, to show respect."

Holt Market

The date the livestock market transferred from the market place to the yard behind the Feathers Hotel remains unknown, but it has certainly been there within the memory span of people interviewed during the compiling of this book.

> With its weekly Friday market, Holt was a fascinating place to live in. Early in the day, farmers began to arrive, animals for sale were driven up the road from far and near, cheapjacks came with their wares and assembled in the market behind the Feathers Hotel, right in the centre of the town – not without its mud, manure and stench; and we often used to walk round the pens to inspect, especially if we were selling poultry or porkers. The town seethed with rare characters, none more outstanding than Old Tom Tipple, a very tall, somewhat notorious gypsy often in trouble with the police. In those days Holt had a Town Crier, one known as 'Carrots' Lake from his shock of red hair. If ever we stopped to hear his 'cry' he invariably seemed to notice us and always finished up with his own variant: 'God save the King, Matt King, the Reverend King, Mrs King and all the little Kings!' Matt King was a well-known churchwarden, a travelling salesman in clothes who drove his handsome horse and trap round the villages and to off-beat farmhouses selling his wares, suits, garments and the like. On occasions I was allowed to accompany him, driving his trap and minding his horse while he was transacting business, a simple but enthralling experience for me. (John King)

Earle Kirby "Market – I can remember them driving cattle through the town and stopping all the traffic. There was only one entrance then – that narrow gap into the Feathers yard, there was no way through from the back like there is now. There was often quite a performance there."

Eva Lord had a good vantage point in her drawing-room on the first floor opposite the market entrance.

Eva Lord "Market day – there'd be donkeys, chickens, geese, sometimes a dog or two, ponies, our sitting-room window is exactly facing the Feathers yard, and my mother, who was confined to a chair for the last years of her life, used to sit there on a Friday watching – the farmers used to wave at her sitting there. All the men went into the Feathers halfway through. Once one of the men got a little bit, er, merry, so they set him on a donkey and the donkey ran away down the town, and on down the Letheringsett Hill. The man in question – I won't name him – was hanging on to the donkey's mane all the way. It sobered him up considerably!"

The Market Place – South Side

Before we continue along the south side of the Market Place in an easterly direction, we should pause to look back and survey the scene. On the left, in the premises now occupied by Spar, is the general store, Culley. Kelly's Directory,1900, lists the proprietor as: Harry Culley, general draper, outfitter and provision merchant, Market Place and at Briston. We already know that Mr Culley lived in the Manor House, and went bankrupt in 1922. These premises were taken over by the International Stores. The sign just beyond the 'Y' in Culley reads 'Feathers Hotel Yard', the entrance to the Friday livestock market. The next building, now Lloyds Bank, is Elden House, where Burrell the basket-maker lived, and where his daughters (presumably), Edith and Hilda Burrell, ran the school attended by Eva Lord. Straight ahead, of course, is the looming presence of Barclays Bank, with the smaller Reliance Printing Works next door, and then Lee. The awnings to the shops on the right are to Neal, watch-maker and cycle agent. Out of shot come Knowles, the tailor and then Gooch.

Early motor car taking up a worrying position in the flow of traffic! Note cart advancing, left.

CT Baker, 1842–1900

Anthony Baker "Mr CT Baker was an exceedingly able man. He not only controlled everything but in addition took a very active part in the working of the business. Nothing great or small was done without his personal knowledge."

CT Bakers

The Baker family justifiably takes pride from the fact that it has traded as ironmongers in Holt since 1782. This represents the longest association with commerce of any family in Holt. In terms of the span of this volume – 1900–1929 – the firm of CT Baker entered the twentieth century in a strong position, as 'a Wholesale and Retail Ironmonger, Builder, Contractor and General Store… at Holt, Fakenham and Sheringham'. Evidence of its scale of operation comes from the following statement: 'A workforce totalling thirty-seven, even if spread between three branches, would be an indication of the substantial size of the business.' We learn this from Anthony Baker, who compiled the comprehensive history of the firm from which we take this information. CT Baker had a son, Charles, and six daughters, five of whom – Ros, Mary, Maud, Nellie and Mabel – were to take an active role in the company in the first quarter of the century. It is true CT Baker had relied on the personal wealth of his wife to fund his expansion, but the business he developed was a thriving concern. Charles qualified as a lawyer and came to realise the benefits of turning the family firm into a limited company; he advised his father accordingly. This process was under way when CT Baker died, in August 1900, at the comparatively young age of fifty-eight; the business then passed to Charles and the change to a limited company was completed. That was probably in itself an advantageous move, but the son appears not to have had the same personal input as his father, nor was he a natural businessman. He was more at ease with municipal affairs, as he was Town Clerk in Sheringham. Sadly, he contracted pneumonia and died just five years later, leaving a widow and two sons, with a third still to be born. On Charles' death, his mother took over as effective Managing Director for the following seven years, and was principal shareholder, owning 5001 of the 5007 shares; she had, through her own financial investment over a considerable period, already been closely involved with the company. She resigned in April,1912, and, two days before her death, her daughter Ros took over as Chairman of Directors.

Anthony Baker now makes this fascinating observation:

"The Company may have been unique in the latter part of 1914 and 1915 in that the Chairman (Ros) and the two other Directors (Mary and Maud) and all the shareholders (Ros, Mary, Nellie, Mabel and Maud) were women. By the end of the twentieth century this would cause little comment but at the time (before women had the suffrage) it would have been considered very strange and unusual."

. T. BAKER, Ltd.,
ON WORKERS,
S, HYDRAULIC & ELECTRICAL ENGINEERS,
Fakenham, and Sheringham.
SPECIAL ATTENTION TO
INAGE & VENTILATION.
tary Work carried out on the latest and most improved scientific principles.
RGES LOW.   PROMPT ATTENTION.
etent Workmen sent to any part.
UILDING REPAIRS PROMPTLY
and CAREFULLY EXECUTED.
LARGE STOCK OF
, RANGES, and all IRONMONGERY GOODS.
cultural, Horticultural & Domestic Machines of every description.
al Repairing Shops for everything

The accompanying advertisement reflects the scope of day-to-day business. At the financial level, the annual dividends declared show a healthy period of trading. The highest (25%) were payable in 1919, 1920 and again in 1924. Throughout these years it was at least 20%, whereas in 1914 it had fallen to 12.5%. No doubt there was considerable trade after World War One, in re-building local infrastructure following the military encampments in the district. However, the family history makes it clear that relationships between the sisters were deteriorating during these years, with 'sides' being taken at Board Meetings. This resulted eventually in a court case in 1925, Ros and Nellie forming one faction, Maud and Mabel another. Mary was in the middle.

In the event, Ros and Nellie won the case, leading to the departure from the company of both Maud and Mabel.

All the while the sisters, none of whom had children, were advancing in years, as were their nephews, the three sons of brother Charles. Jim (born 1903) joined the firm in 1927, having completed training and apprenticeship in Huntingdon and Maidstone. In 1928 he took over as Manager of the Sheringham shop, and by 1931 was General Manager of the company.

Larners

George and Harriet Larner opened shop in Market Place in 1872. Two sons, Bruce and Malcolm ran the shop during the early years of the twentieth century. Bruce's daughter Margaret married John Clarke; they ran the shop until selling to CT Baker Ltd. No more information has come to light as yet, but Eva Lord, whose father ran FW Bakers, makes these observations.

Eva Lord "Bruce Larner and Malcolm Larner, brothers, I think. Malcolm had the grocery side, Bruce the drapery. My father was the other draper in the town, they never cribbed on each other's sales – there was great 'esprit de corps' among them all. My father catered for the working-class, you see, while Bruce Larner's customers were rather more prosperous. One side of the shop was drapery, and the other side was grocery. Malcolm was a jolly old boy, but Bruce was a miserable man. I won't tell you what we used to call him, 'cos I never know what you're going to put in your stories..."

Robinson's Garage

Sadly, we do not as yet have a photo of these premises, which were in the building next to Larners. However, John Turner, whose father ran the business soon after it started in the early twenties, has some memories.

John Turner "My father went to war in 1914, he was taken prisoner on the Somme, and when he came out, he went into the motor trade with Elsdens. Then he got together with some farmer friends, and they set up Robinson's garage – lovely old place to be, very well equipped, had its full share of customers, we were very proud of it. My father was also the Captain of the Holt Fire Brigade; this worked in very nicely with the garage, of course, because whenever they had a fire, away they had to go. It was all voluntary, then – the station was in the Shirehall Plain, right in the corner – it had great difficulty in housing the fire engine, which was built at Robinson's garage by my father and a very good man we had there, Bruce Wasey. It was built on an old Vulcan chassis. This proved too big for the existing station – that's why they moved to the new one in the former Primitive Methodist Chapel in Chapel Yard."

Cinema!

One of their customers, a certain CW Jex, had already made use of a run-down building at the rear of the premises to open a cinema – not how we may conceive of such a building these days, however!

Earle Kirby "There was a cinema to the back of Robinson's garage – not really a cinema in the first instance, more a place to show slides. My father told me, 'We hadn't been in Holt long when I decided to take your mum to the cinema one night. When we got in there – it was a tin shed in the yard behind the garage – there weren't rows of fixed seats, they had loose chairs, hard seats were cheaper than the wicker chairs. When it rained, the corrugated iron roof rattled and leaked, so you had to move your chairs about to avoid the spots of water!' They'd been used to town life, so they wondered what they'd come to! That really amused my father."

n Jarvis "Being a silent ma, the projector had a e wheel which had to be ed by hand. My great- e Jack was one of the ectionists, and if he ted to get off early to his girlfriend, he would the wheel a bit faster!"

Working my way through the Checkley albums in the Norfolk Record Office, I came across the name that Mr Jex created for his establishment: The Electric Pavilion! But on reflection, it was a canny choice of site; mains electricity did not come to Holt until the early thirties. Before then, power was generated by small internal combustion engines, serviced by... Robinson's garage.

The Market Place – North Side

The view on the right was taken from the end of Station Road. The War Memorial has replaced Blind Sam, removed to Obelisk Plain. The top of the water tower may be seen far left above the roofs of Gooch the chemist, and FS Ransom, William Thomas, boot and shoe maker (Kelly 1900).

Tucked behind the shoe shop (Siddalls are still selling shoes from this site!), is the pretty, small building, now the legal firm of Butcher Andrews. Jane Hales recalls: 'An exception to old buildings is the house occupied by Mr T Savory, clerk, which replaced a house where lived Mrs Williamson in the last two decades of the nineteenth century. She was a herbalist and drove out into the country in her donkey cart to collect specimens.' Their neighbours were the Clares; Edith Pointin continues with a none too flattering recollection. 'Next was the Post Office. Mr and Mrs Clare ran this one side and sold stationery the other. I well remember they had a bead curtain between their room and it always fascinated us children. I remember, too, my sister Lillian taking me in when I had whooping cough and Mrs Clare shouted, 'Take that child out of here.' They were a miserable old couple.'

Edith Pointin "Then came a wonderful shoe shop owned by Mr Ransom. He employed several men to repair shoes; they were always busy."

The next positive identification is the International Stores, (now the Alliance and Leicester), recalled by Edith Pointin. 'Just through was the International Stores. How well I remember going there in the time of the First World War. They sold a strange substance. I believe it was called coconut butter, off the ration.' When Culley's closed, the International Stores moved across the Market Place; Shipp's Cycles took its place.

The International stores opened in 1910.

On the far right of the photo of the North side of the Market Place is a shop under the ownership of GW Starling. A magnifying glass reveals the following: the painted sign above the window reads: 'Tobacco, Pipes, Cigarettes, Stationery, Lending Library'. Cadbury's chocolate is clearly a favoured product, as its name appears, large or small, in several places. On the wall to the right of the window, we may read: 'The Library, read the latest novels'; while between the small window and the doorway are the words 'Best Paper, Holt News'.

Blind Sam

We now find the tall, elegant lamp standard, known familiarly as Blind Sam, in Obelisk Plain, but its first location was the Market Place. Here is its story.

The Queen Victoria Jubilee Lantern stood in the Market Place between 1887 and 1921, when it was moved to Obelisk Plain to make way for the War Memorial. When it was first erected it served a double function: first, to give illumination to the Market Place, and second it was linked to the water supply.

Drinking water was available through the provision of water bowls set on two sides of the column; cast-iron cups, attached by chains at a convenient height, could be dipped into these bowls. As for the light – powered by the town's gas supply, of course – this sadly proved to be of intermittent efficiency only, leading to its nickname, 'Blind Sam'. In the early 1990s, the Holt History Group started a project to restore the column to its former glory, as the lantern itself had been missing for years. Research was undertaken, resulting in the discovery of a pattern in the catalogue of Walter MacFarlane's Saracen Foundry at Possil, Glasgow. This firm was 'rated as being one of the finest in the decorative branch of iron-founding' with some notable credits, particularly in British Empire lands. In choosing this company to create the dual-purpose, extra-special lamp standard to honour Queen Victoria's Golden Jubilee, the citizens of Holt made a shrewd choice; moreover, we are now fortunate to be able to enjoy it restored to its original beauty.

BLIND SAM

THE
QUEEN VICTORIA
JUBILEE
LANTERN

John Chapman and his family/staff outside their bakery.

Fish Hill

Sad to say, we have not seen any photo of this attractive corner of Holt, apart from this one of the Chapman bakery at the far end. It is clear that the buildings on the left are homes, not shops. We are shortly to read of Henry Hobart's childhood memories – he lived in the house where the two young ladies are standing.

A Holt Childhood – Henry Hobart

Henry Hobart "I grew up on Fish Hill, the eldest of seven children, in the house that is now a sewing shop. I knew the Revd Field, who was a housemaster of the Old School House. He said to me, 'The grounds of the Old School House are free to you in the school holiday, I hold you responsible.' He was a proper gentleman. I became a Scout at the Scout hut up near the church – or perhaps I was a Cub there; Ronnie Byford was the Cub master."

Barber Brown surveys the scene from the doorway of his barber's shop, with his apprentice Harry McMahon, from the Star Inn.

Henry talks about his neighbours and the shops in his vicinity.

"The International Stores came next to my grandmother, then moved a year or two later; Shipp bought this. The Green family was next door to me; later, my aunt bought that house and made it into a fish shop. Then there was Waller, the pork butcher, Mrs Bond the fruiterer – she had a big family actually, seven kids; I think her husband was killed in the war. I always remember her, as she was had up two or three times for watering the milk. The there was a man called Sapy who sold sweets. The little building further along was Nicholls the barbers – then it became Harry West's fish shop. Herbert Strutt had the place that's now Feeney's. Before he moved in, it was a barbers' shop, manned by Brown. Two or three years later there were three barber's shops there, because Jarrold took over the shop which had been Starlings – now it's a florist. Earlier, it had belonged to Preston..."

Henry's valiant attempt to summarise the changes in his locality emphasises the problems of charting the detailed history of family and commercial life in the town! We can arrive at the actual dates of such small shifts only if we chance upon the right combination of data – house deeds, census information, family archives, town directories, personal letters, photos. Henry's next revelation leaves us wondering…

"Bond the solicitor had a place on the corner of Church Lane, where the Owl Tea Room is; I remember there were seven or eight books lying on the floor, and they were all the History of Holt – and I've often wondered and wondered what happened to those books. Perhaps there were only three or four – everything was handwritten in them. That's the same place as during the First World War a horse and wagon went straight through his window – driver was killed. I was down on the pavement on the opposite side of the road – people were shouting – the man tried to leap off the horse…"

Those readers of a sensitive disposition should not read the next paragraph.

"The dog in the photo (left) was called Spot, and he belonged to Alice, my aunt, my mother's sister. He's the only dog I knew that would kill snakes on the Lowes.

Near the end of his life, my father and grandfather had been talking about putting the old dog down. The next day, they heard from Munson, the stationmaster, who said, 'If ever I saw a dog commit suicide, I've just seen it. Spot stood on the railway line and let the train take his head off. He's been here hundreds of times, he knows the trains better than I do.' Makes you wonder, doesn't it?"

Later in his childhood, Henry and his friends took to the open spaces.

"I used to live on the Lowes in the summer holidays. Ernest Abrams, George Wright, we dug a dugout near Soldiers' Pit, we lined it with six-inch saplings from the wood at the back, we lined the roof. One day, we found a box of hand grenades, which we threw in the Pit at first; but then we thought about it, and thought we should go to police to tell them. I used to catch adders on there, and get ten bob each for adder skins from Gresham's – Williamson was the man. The Lowes meant something to us, you know."

One man stands out.

"And then there was Carrot Lake the town crier, an ex-Army man – he had a really terrific voice on him. I was once waiting at the top of the Hill to go footballing – that was before Blind Sam was down there. There were four or five of us standing there, when a big car drew up. It was one of those early cars where the chauffeur was separate from the rest of the interior. Inside, there was a very prosperous-looking man, who pulled the window down and shouted out to Carrot Lake, 'Do I take this road to Norwich, my good man?' Carrot replied, 'You can take it wherever you like, it doesn't belong to me!' I heard people say that he was the only man who could read out the Army regulations without hesitation, take him about three-quarters of an hour."

Other memories.

"Dr Skrimshire had me go to hospital and have adenoids out – within four years I started to go deaf. I didn't know him give anything but aspirins; but every time I went to see him he gave me sixpence. He had four big bottles of medicines in his surgery. Once, when I was at Fakenham, three or four of us went to his orchard and pinched his apples. Well, I was up a tree, and the gardener Graveling saw me – but my school cap dropped off. The others ran away, of course. I was taken to see Dr Skrimshire. And this is what he said to me: 'If you want apples, come in the front door!' Ever such a kind man, he was – and he gave me a shilling! His apples weren't that good, either!"

Holt Fair

Jane Hales That a market was held here is one of the oldest facts we know about Holt, for it is mentioned in the Domesday Book. Radford writes, 'markets were originally held outside a church on holy days, when people were assembled for divine service.' Beside the present Market Place, a map of 1800 shows a corn market on the Shirehall Plain, and before that there had been a yarn market there. At the beginning of the nineteenth century, market was held on a Saturday, but it was later moved to Friday. Holt Fair Days were April 25th and November 25th. Fair days were great events. At the end of the nineteenth century, the pleasure fair was held along the north side of the Market Place, with a menagerie in the middle. A little boy in a house nearby shivered in his bed at the roaring of lions and tigers. He remembers, too, the Dutch Auction on Fish Hill. A dealer in pottery held up an object, but, unable to get a satisfactory bid, cast it to the ground, where it broke all to pieces. People thronged in from surrounding parishes, for the fair was a great event. But shopkeepers got annoyed at all the excitement outside their doors. The couple at the Post Office-cum-stationers complained, and eventually, at the beginning of this century, the fair was moved. There was no through traffic problem in those days, and the Cromer Road entrance to the Market Place was blocked with stalls, and horses and carts had to use the Bull Street instead. The Hempstead Road entrance was left open. On the Fairstead, at the end of New Street, were horses, donkeys, bullocks, sheep, and once an elephant. The Feathers Yard was used for fat stock.

Holt Fair Day is always cold, so don't expect continuous warm spring weather till after April 25th, for the Fair Day is in the midst of the blackthorn winter. It is also St Mark's Day, which is packed with folklore...

Chapter 6

Holt became almost a garrison town
throughout the war. (Dallas Wynne Wilson.)

How the War came to Holt

Early August, 1914, and devastating news arrived in Holt in a young man's hand. At that stage, the Old School House in the Market Place was a boarding-house for the Junior School of Gresham's, and Dallas Wynne Wilson was its housemaster. He recalled the moment in his memoirs.

I note that the weather on Tuesday August 4th was showery in the afternoon. About midnight I went into the town to Rounce & Wortley's Stationery Shop, where news was to be posted. It came from Cromer by a motorcyclist, A Moulton, one of our day boys. It was read out – the fateful message that England had declared war against Germany at 11 pm. There was a crowd in the street and an outburst of cheering, and I remember our school doctor, Kentish Wright, shouting, 'Don't cheer; you don't know what you are in for!' All that night there was noise and excitement: boy Scouts were cycling about calling up reservists and territorials. I can't remember if any of them went off that night.

We are incredibly fortunate to have access to this first-hand account of Holt's experience of war. How else would we know how those days actually were?

Wednesday (an extra bank holiday) was showery and thundery. A day of rumours, unrest. We expected a naval battle off our coast! My brother-in-law, Christopher Hughes, was with us, and I went up, late at night, to the high fire staircase on our new buildings and listened for that noise of guns at sea, and we almost persuaded ourselves that we could hear them.

A sea battle, off Salthouse, really?

So strong were the rumours of a naval battle next day, (Thursday, August 6th) that Miller and I summoned all the principal people of Holt to a meeting in my school dining-hall, that day, to arrange for reception of the wounded. I was elected Chairman and we formed a number of committees for transport, ambulance work etc, and arranged for the loan of beds, bedding and other necessaries, and the next day I telephoned to the Governors of the School (the Headmaster had gone away and we could not get him) and obtained permission to use the school dormitories for temporary hospitals!

That was not all.

One morning we woke up to find the village market place in front of my house full of soldiers. They had been brought from Sussex in taxicabs, reminding one of General Manouny's similar action before the battle of Marne! We saw a lot of officers and particularly their CO, Colonel Holmes, a brother I believe of the Archdeacon of London. They were the forerunners of a very large number of soldiers, and Holt became almost a

garrison town throughout the war. Actually the first soldiers I saw were a day or two after August 4th, when cyclists from some place along the coast were sent over to Weybourne where they dug a few trenches on the cliff (about a foot off the edge, I noticed, which did not seem to promise much protection). Some of us cycled over from Holt to take them cakes and jam and other small delicacies. They were really the first defenders of the country in action that we had met.

Holt – a garrison town! Not just the Market Place. John King:

Immediately our area was bustling with troops and troop movements. The field opposite our front gate was filled with artillery, guns and their limber carriages, troops and tents; and our dining-room was handed over to the commanding officers, who slept in it in their camp-beds. Throughout the war, our parents organised musical soirées or tea-parties, chiefly for the officers; but the other ranks were not neglected.

Housemaster Wynne Wilson had other worries.

The autumn of 1914 was an anxious time for us schoolmasters. I had a household of fifty small boys under 14, and three under 6, and we were told that in case of a raid we might have to evacuate the place at two or three hours' notice. In fact we were so near the coast that the first indication might have been a shell plump in the middle of town. My instructions were that in such a case we were to go westward and keep to byroads or go across country, leaving the main roads free for troops, and make our way to Kings Lynn. Fancy doing that with such a household in the middle of a bitter November night!

The King family had now been resident in Holt for five years. The eldest, Francis, recalls the immediate impact of the declaration of war. Francis King:

The big upheaval for Holt as for everywhere else came with World War One. I remember that father, mother and we, the children, were having a picnic upon the glebe field above the wood when someone came to tell us that war had been declared. In a day or two a regiment appeared (was it the Scot's Greys under General Dorrien?) and settled down in fields near and around Holt, at the Oddy's, at Holt Lodge, and immediately opposite our front gate. But they soon left for France. During the war, many soldiers came to the house. Two fixed themselves in my memory, an artist called Codner and Maurice Cole the pianist.

Edith Pointin, living in her home at the town end of New Street, was a girl of six at this time.

Edith Pointin "I well remember the day World War One started, and heard my dad say it wouldn't last long. Each household was sent a leaflet telling that, should the Germans land at Weybourne, we were all to go to Holt Hills and take just the things we needed most. When my mother took me to see a Mrs Bass, whose husband was Head Gardener at Woodlands, part of Gresham's school, she was told, 'I've packed all my jam' – a mere hundred jars! When Mother told Dad they had a real laugh. Later, soldiers flooded into Holt, and those who had room had to have them. I think the three we had were Welsh, as they called each other Taffey. After one week they

went to the front and a week or so later, my mother was crying. She said all those young boys had been killed. We had various soldiers after that and for quite a time the Duke of Cornwall. He had the two best rooms and Mother cooked his meals. He was the CO of that group. His valet would come twice a day to clean his shoes and buttons, and press his suits. Twice a week he had a can of cream brought up by train all the way from Devon. It was the valet's job to bring it up the street, and I can see him now carrying it by its thin wire handle. I pinched many a spoonful my mother didn't know about! One day Mother left his door open whilst she was making up the fire and I peeped in. He called, 'And what have you been learning at school today?' I said, 'A poem called 'Mr Nobody',' to which he said, 'Come in and say it to me.' Which I did, and he gave me two pence – a fortune in those days."

Eva Lord's home above her father's shop had capacious attics, soon to be commandeered by the military.

Eva Lord "We had about three attics, one large attic, slept in by fourteen soldiers at the outbreak of the first war, just to sleep. At that particular time, my father had a garden down by the Spout Hills, and we had some marvellous fruit trees, and all the apples and pears were laid out on straw in this large attic. Everybody had to jump to and work hard to take up that fruit again! And the sergeant-major of the regiment – Sergeant-Major Diggle, a short, fat man – came and said, 'Yes ,ma'am, you can take fourteen soldiers here to sleep'. I don't think they stayed very long, probably about a month, and then they were sent abroad, you see. But there are about twelve stairs going up to this attic; every night about ten o'clock you heard all this marching up the stairs. My mother was paid fourteen shillings a week for that, and she thought it was riches. We had a little wash-house at the end of our yard, with a copper, and that's where they had to have a bath. Of course we didn't have a bathroom."

We are bound to ask a fundamental question – why so much troop incursion, in this far curve of the land?

The Riddle of the Sands

The answer lies in the pages of this spy novel, written by Erskine Childers, and

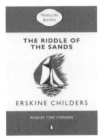

published early in the 1900s. This truly is an instance where an i n d i v i d u a l ' s imagination, expressed through fiction, affected policy at national level – military, in this case. The novel played with the idea of a possible German naval force assembling on the Friesland coast, with one view in mind – to invade Britain. In a way, the novel gave form to the growing fears in the public mind, in the early years of the century, about the eventual outcome of Germany's hostile international stance. Here is a succinct overview:

> The shock of this book on its release a century ago, set in the years of European tension leading up to the First World War, caused a sensation in Britain by successfully analysing what in military terms can only be called Germany's increasingly 'aggressive posture'. Childers did this in a story which broke new ground, as it is generally agreed to be the first straight modern spy thriller, even more remarkable for it being a first novel.

The particular effect on Holt and its environs was due to a key geographical factor about the local coastline, namely that there is deep water off Weybourne.

Dallas Wynne Wilson wrote:

> This place, Weybourne, had always been regarded as a possible landing place for an invader, as there is deep water right up to the pebble beach; probably Danish and Saxon invaders had landed on this shore. There is a current local rhyme:

> He who would Old England win
> Must at Weybourne Hope begin.

John King, writing in the family memoir in the 1980s, has these comments on the whole matter.

> While it is true to say we suffered from none of the privations of war, we were intensely aware of war from its outset. An old rhyme of which various versions exist, states: according to FHK (Francis King) "He who would England win, Must at Weybourne hopp begin." And according to PGCK (Philip King) "Who would Old England win, Must at Weybourne Bight begin"; and Churchill quotes a slightly different version. The fact of the matter is that ever since *The Riddle of the Sands* by Erskine Childers (partly instrumental in the founding of the RNVR) the possibility of invasion of the East Coast had been kept under strict surveillance, for there is deep water off Weybourne. The Lowes, a fine heathland where as schoolboys after the war we used to catch lizards, adders and newts, was put out of bounds so that grenade practice and shooting ranges could be established. Even in 1915 or '16 when we were at West Runton, the normal tracks to the beach were denied us because of coastal defence. Possible invasion was taken as a serious threat.'

CORRESPONDANCE

To my Loving
Wife from
Your loving
Husband
Fred

ADRESSE

Mrs F Green
Fish Hills
Holt
Norfolk
England

Fred Green, standing third from the left, sent greetings to his wife from the front.

Young men enlist

Eva Lord watched her brother go out and come back years later.

Eva Lord "My brother Leslie was seventeen and a half and the age to enlist was eighteen, but the boys were all anxious to go, and he gave his age as eighteen. He was sent to the Britannia Barracks in Norwich. During his training there he was in the 2nd Norfolks. We went up to see him, I was about five years old at the time, and I can just remember bumping along to Norwich in this old Ford. From there he was sent on to Colchester, where he finished his training, and then abroad to Salonika, and from there on to Mesopotamia. He went from boy to man in about six months, thoroughly disillusioned. He had dysentery, malaria, and after Mesopotamia he went on to India for three years. He was away about four and a half years. I can remember the night he came back to Holt, with all his photographs and things. After a rest and holiday he came and helped my father in the shop."

Soldiers at Holt Camp.

Men line up.

Zeppelins

North Norfolk was subject to enemy attack from the air, in the form of Zeppelin raids, with the first airship raid on Britain taking place on the night of 19 January 1915. Zeppelins of the Imperial German Navy Airship Division dropped bombs on Great Yarmouth and King's Lynn, killing five people. In an attempt to intercept the raiders, The Royal Flying Corps took to the skies, but the two aircraft failed in their bid. The very sight of this structure must have been truly awe-inspiring, at a time when the aeroplane was an extreme rarity. But in the dark of night, 19 January, huge cigar-shaped threats droned towards them. And what were they, these Zeppelins? Each airship contained nineteen individual gas-filled bags and a crew of twenty-one, housed in two gondolas slung beneath their enormous structures. Three motors enabled them to reach speeds of 50 mph (80 kph). At this stage in the evolution of air travel, Zeppelins were the ultimate flying machine both in range and length of time they could stay airborne. However, filled as they were with hydrogen, any leak formed an explosive mixture with air; while manoeuvring near the ground, collisions were sometimes devastating. During the entire war 56 tons of bombs fell on London and 214 tons elsewhere. There were several raids on Norfolk, but the intended destination, Norwich, was never located. It seems difficult to credit now, but the sophistication of the airship itself was accompanied by an extremely basic – and chancy – technique for closing in on the target. Up in the sky they had maps while down on the ground they had... accomplice cars, fitted with extra-powerful headlights, driven by... 'spies'. Eye-witness reports 'tell stories of spies signalling out to sea prior to the night of the raids and of powerful cars leading Zeppelins to their targets along country lanes.'

Britain eventually responded to the Zeppelins with its own airship, the Pulham Pigs.

For the experience of Holt people, we have the expert witness of Dallas Wynne Wilson.

It was in January 1915 that the first Zeppelin raid took place and we were among the first people to see or hear them when they first came over England. We were told at Holt that a Zeppelin was hovering off Sheringham: they had a 4.7 gun on the links there, but I believe its elevation was not great enough and its use would have meant considerable retaliation on the town. As it was, they dropped two or three small bombs, which were the first actually dropped on English soil. At about eight o'clock they came over us at Holt, and we put out all lights. I think there must have been plenty visible in town as I went out and found a big iron-mongers shop lit up as usual, and went in and turned out every gas jet. The little boys in my boarding house (I had the junior house, of boys under fourteen) were on the whole more excited than alarmed. About seven o'clock I was out in the town and saw a number of bright flashes to the northwest accompanied by explosions. Later I found that these came from a Zeppelin which had dropped a number of bombs about two miles off us in the Glaven Valley, where they were trying to locate a searchlight or an anti-aircraft gun. Actually the bombs all fell around a farmhouse, killing one or two sheep and a turkey, and dislodging some tiles. Next day the school repaired thither en masse to inspect the damage, and the boys searched the small craters for bits of bombs; they collected from round the farm quite a large store of old scrap iron, which had probably lain there for decades. I remember taking a parcel of sweets down for the small children at the farmhouse, who had of course been very much frightened. The Zeppelin also dropped a few bombs in Sir Alfred Jodrell's Park at Bayfield.

Francis King remembered that night, too:

The most dramatic event I can remember was of a Zeppelin, in early evening but already dark, which sounded as if it had lost its way. I was on my way back from school and stopped outside Watson's cottage (St John's Cottage – Ed) to listen to the high up, bumbling sound of its engines. Shortly afterwards it dropped a stick of bombs, probably aiming at a small aerodrome at Bayfield, on the Cley road, just opposite the turning on to Salthouse Heath. The damage to a farm building at Bayfield Brecks was minimal; and the next day, with other Gresham boys, I was down there gathering bits of bombs as souvenirs. My find was a grooved all-metal aerial dart.

Dallas Wynne Wilson enrolled as a special constable in the town.

During the war I was out on special constable duty twenty-nine times but never saw a Zeppelin though I heard them nearly every time. Generally I was at supper when there would be a ring at the front door and a message was brought in from the Superintendent at the Police Station, 'Field Marshal's warning', and off I had to go to look after lights. Several times this duty took one most of the

night. I say I never saw a Zeppelin, but on two occasions I saw the light of the destruction of one. Once it was about a quarter past 1 am when we saw a bright light to the southeast, and I remarked: 'They have hit a gasometer this time'. It turned out to be the destruction of the Zeppelin at Cuffley, over 100 miles away. As it was destroyed at about 6000 feet I suppose to see it was quite possible, as one would see a mountain 6000 feet high a hundred miles away in flat country.

He continues with this observation.

It was curious on Zeppelin nights that the

Just "a line" from HOLT.

earliest warning was given by the pheasants in the many coverts round Holt. Sometimes when we got very weary of patrolling the town, we turned into the police station and sat awhile in a darkened room with the Superintendent. He had a window in the room which recorded the slightest distant vibration, and its rattle was a signal to turn us out. On these nights the trains were often halted until the raids were over. All their windows were closely shielded, or lights put out.

John King recalls a Zeppelin raid:

There were few alarms and excursions; but two incidents stand out in my memory. At Bayfield there was a small fighter aerodrome to which we sometimes walked in the hopes of watching Sopwiths take off and land. Overall, there was not much activity; but one sunny afternoon when we were catching minnows, we suddenly saw a balloon rise above the trees in Bayfield's direction. Most of us let out a scream of fear. This must be a German Zeppelin! However, our fears were soon allayed, but momentarily the war was brought very near to us. We did in fact hear a Zeppelin. One night when we were all fast asleep, father thought it wise to wake us up – there must have been at least five of us, four in the night nursery and Francis in the dressing-room which led off it – to see the Zeppelin. We all crammed and huddled in the window to listen, and clearly heard its engines, but in considerable trepidation began to whimper with alarm. Father intuitively knew how to deal with the matter. 'If you don't all stop crying,' he said in authoritative tones, 'you'll all go back to bed and you won't see the Zeppelin when it comes! This put an end to our crying if not to our fears. Though we could not see it, we heard the humming of its engines clearly. This Zeppelin was, I believe, shot down in Yorkshire.

Dallas Wynne Wilson:

Later in the war anti-aircraft guns and searchlights were installed on Kelling Heath. The former were never used, but the latter were a constant pleasure to watch criss-crossing each other across the sky. On that coast, standing high, is the beautiful church of Blakeney, and its tall tower was said to be a landmark by which the Zeppelins made their way in. I believe it was seriously suggested that this church tower should be taken down and put up somewhere else, and so mislead the Zeppelins!

Dallas Wynne Wilson had other tasks as well.

One of the duties that occasionally fell to us was to put stray members of the military on their way home. I remember one who had evidently visited the laundry (and also other places!) who was setting a trail by dropping socks and handkerchiefs as he went. One's duties as a constable were not very onerous. At the beginning of the war I had to go out with another from midnight to 3am, and this on a raw November night was not enjoyable. All we had to do then was to patrol streets and look under certain bridges to see that there were no explosives. After January 1915, when the first Zeppelin raid had occurred, it was our business to see that no lights were shown, and this was more interesting. I remember one night calling at a house, which was the headquarters of one of the regiments, as the blind in front was not fully drawn up. I was soundly cursed by a Major for my d----d impertinence, but I stuck to it and stayed till the blind was pulled down.

Holt Camp.

THERE'S an isolated, desolated spot I'd like to mention,
  Where all you hear is "Stand at Ease," "Slope Arms,"
    "Quick March, ' " Attention,"
It's miles away from anywhere, by Gad, it is a rum'un,
A chap lived there for fifty years and never saw a woman.
There's only two lamps in the place, so tell it to your mother,
The postman carries one, and the policeman has the other,
And if you want a jolly night, and do not care a jot,
You take a ride upon the car, the car they haven't got.
There are lots of little huts, all dotted here and there,
For those who have to live inside, I've offered many a prayer,
Inside the huts, there's RATS as big as any Nanny Goat,
Last night a soldier saw One Fitting on his Overcoat.
For Breakfast every morning, just like Old Mother Hubbard,
You Double round the bloomin' Hut and jump up at the cupboard
Sometimes you get bacon, and sometimes "lively" cheese,
That forms Platoon upon your plate, Orders Arms and Stands
  at Ease.
It's sludge up to the eyebrows, you get it in your ears,
But into it you've got to go without a sign of fear,
And when you've had a bath of sludge, you just set to and groom,
And get cleaned up for next Parade, or else it's "Orderly Room."
Week in, week out, from morn till night, with full Pack and a rifle,
Like Jack and Jill, you climb the hills, of course that's just a trifle,
"Slope Arms," "Fix Bayonets," then "Present" they fairly put
  you through it.
And as you stagger to your hut, the Sergeant shouts "Jump to it."
There's another kind of drill, especially invented for the Army,
I think they call it Swedish, and it nearly drives you barmy ;
This blinking drill it does you good, it makes your bones so tender
You can coil yourself up like a snake and crawl beneath the fender
With tunics, boots and putties off, you quickly get the habit,
You gallop up and down the hills just like a blooming rabbit,
"Heads Backward Bend," "Arms Upward Stretch," "Heels
  Raise," then "Ranks Change Places,"
And later on they make you put your kneecaps where your face is.
Now when this War is over and we've captured Kaiser Billy,
To shoot him would be merciful and absolutely silly,
Just send him down to HOLT, among the rats and clay,
And I'll bet it won't be long before he droops and fades away
  BUT WE'RE STILL "MERRY AND BRIGHT."

From   *(All rights reserved.)*

Almanack 1916

The following dated extracts each give us an insight into the nature of the times. We get a sense, too, of the attitudes and sensibilities of Holt people in these years, not forgetting their interests and pursuits!

War there may be, but life in Holt carried on, not as normal, but with necessary adjustments. We start with the end of an era for cricket-lovers – and news of a remarkable match in Letheringsett many years before.

7 January 1915. Richard Pilch of Norwich, and formerly of Holt, a nephew of the famous Fuller Pilch, passed away rather suddenly but quite peacefully. He was 88 years of age, and up to the last, possessed good health, enjoying much more activity than the great majority of people who attain such an advanced age. His cricket recollections went back so far that to the present generation they must seem almost legendary. The district round about Holt was a great cricket country,

on July 21st, 1846 between Holt and Letheringsett, and the side composed of the eleven brothers Colman. There was a lot of good cricket in Norfolk seventy years ago, and Holt was an important centre, some of the big men of the day coming down.

14 January 1915. The noble art of the gloves is as popular as ever; this was evidenced by the large audience at the Town Hall on that night, when, after the ordinary entertainment given by the "Pelicans", a boxing match took place between Mr Griffithes-Moss, proprietor of the Pelicans and Trooper Frank Goddard, late trainer of Bombardier Wells. The contest was ten rounds of two minutes and some pretty play resulted. Mr Griffiths-Moss is a really first-class amateur, but Goddard had a very great advantage in years, and was in the pink of condition. The finish came in the sixth round, after a clever display on the part of both men.

19 February 1915. An excellent concert took place in the Concert Hall under the patronage and attendance of the officers of the Sixth (Cyclists) Sussex. Corporal Jones was responsible for the programme, and in addition to men of the regiment he was fortunate enough to secure the service of some of the 'Vanities', who were performing in the town. An excellent programme was submitted, and judging by the generous meed of applause given to the various artistes, it earned the appreciation of the large audience.

Kissing in Norfolk!

I have just finished a tour round the County, and have come to the conclusion that Norfolk Girls make kissing a fine art. This is my experience :

CROMER Girls close their eyes, and dreamily suggest some more secluded spot.

HOLT Girls cling very tightly and keep murmuring, "Just once more."

MUNDESLEY Girls try to look very stern, squeeze your hand, and afterwards tell you that "You ought to be ashamed of yourself."

NORTH WALSHAM Girls make a meal of it, and murmur, "Nothing shall come between us."

SHERINGHAM Girls throw their arms round your neck and tell you "The more you do it, the better they love you."

WORSTEAD Girls become very excited, try to bite your ear, and leave you an absolute wreck.

I hear that you have quite a style of your own.

and even now one hears from time to time of the prowess of the men who played at Holt, Cley, Letheringsett, Brinton, Aldborough, Holkham and other places. Pilch's skill was early recognised and he was in great request for matches which in their day aroused a lot of attention in sporting circles. Pilch was the last survivor of a game played at Letheringsett Hall

1 March 1915. A meeting of the Committee of the Literary Institute was held. Mr D E Leggatt was in the chair. At the outset, Mr Leggatt referred, in feeling terms, to the great loss sustained by the death of their late secretary Mr F T Hutchens. Mr Hutchens, he said, was one of the oldest of their members, having been a member for over forty years,

Soldiers off duty, girls on parade. We can name the lady on the left as Hilda Sophia Waller.

and for several years past he had acted as Hon. Secretary, and no-one could have carried out the duties better than he did. He devoted a great deal of time to the work, although it was largely a matter of love.

7 March 1915. A crowded meeting of women and girls was held in the Concert Hall, on behalf of the League of Honour. Mrs Hart was in the chair, supported by the rectors of Holt and Letheringsett, and a ladies' choir of the British Women's Temperance Association who led the singing of a war hymn. The Bishop of Norwich spoke with great earnestness and sympathy of the great part that fell to the girls in the war. Miss Mayers representing the League, further explained its objects and methods. A large number of names were given in at the close of the meeting.

17 March 1915. The body of Lance Corporal William Charles Fifield of the Motorcyclists Section, Sixth Battalion, Royal Sussex Regiment, who was killed on the 14th at Stradsett was brought to Holt on the 17th, and lay in the parish church all night. The coffin was draped with the Union Jack, and on it were placed the deceased's cap, belt and revolver. On the 18th there was a service in the parish church conducted the Revd HA King. Two companies of the Sixth Battalion Royal Sussex Regiment, with the corporals and drivers of the whole battalion were present. The pall bearers were the motorcyclists of the Battalion. As the cortège left the church, the dead march from 'Saul' was played. The coffin was placed on a gun carriage and preceded by a guard of honour under Sgt Corney and Cpl Gringer and the choir, and followed by the men of the Battalion, it was taken to the railway station, where it was placed on the 11.40 train en route for Brighton, where the funeral took place on the 19th.

21 April 1915. After a stay of some months in the town, the Sixth (Cyclists') Battalion of the Royal Sussex Regiment departed. The Sussex men had made themselves, by their exemplary behaviour, warm favourites of the townsfolk and the station was thronged with people bidding the soldiers good-bye and wishing them Bon Voyage. From Col Holmes downwards all expressed their gratitude to their Holt friends for the cordial way they had been treated during their stay. The ladies of the canteen saw that the men had suitable refreshment before they left. Col Holmes acknowledged the kindness of the townsfolk

DON'T WORRY---I'm quite Comfortable at HOLT CAMP.

in an appreciative letter of thanks to Mr M Pearson, chairman of the Parish Council.

20 June 1915. The first of the regular series of war intercession services was held. After evening service the congregation, preceded by the rector and the choir, walked to the Market Place, where two hymns were sung and intercessory prayers offered. The service was most orderly and reverent, and undoubtedly made an impression upon those taking part in it, and upon those who witnessed it.

14 July 1915. The 14th was 'French Day', and a large number of persons in Holt displaying the Tricolour testified to the unsparing efforts of the Misses Reid to make the day a success. It is expected a goodly sum will be forwarded to headquarters as a result of their praiseworthy action.

3 August 1915. A meeting under the auspices of the Central Volunteer Training Corps was held in the Shirehall. Mr SS Burroughes was voted to the chair, the room was crowded. Colonel Francis, commanding the 5th (Coast) Battalion Norfolk Volunteers was the first speaker. He said the object of that meeting was to raise a platoon for Holt, to be attached to the B Company of the Battalion. If they succeeded in forming a platoon, they would form part of the Cromer company. On the motion of Dr HF Skrimshire, seconded by Mr HR Tyler, it was agreed to form a platoon in Holt. And it was furthermore agreed that Major Dalton be appointed platoon commander. About forty of those present handed their names in to Mr Bond, Hon Secretary at the conclusion of the meeting.

2 September 1915. The Holt Volunteers were inspected by Colonel Francis. After assembling at Kenwyn, they marched to the Old School House cricket ground, where they were drilled by Major Dalton. Colonel Francis, in addressing the men, said he was agreeably surprised to find what progress they had made in the short time since their formation, and he was proud to see so many turn out. He hoped they would be ultimately recognised by the government, and suitably armed and equipped for the work they had undertaken to do.

16 September 1915. Following a suggestion made at the meeting of the Parish Council to close the business places at an earlier hour, a meeting of the tradespeople of the town was held in the Shirehall. Mr TM Larner presided over a representative gathering of the trades-people. The meeting had been organised by Mr DC Oddy and Mr FW Baker. After an exhaustive discussion, Mr H Bond proposed, and Mr RC Lewis seconded a resolution, that 'we the tradespeople of the town of Holt hereby undertake to effectually keep our lights sufficiently darkened and call upon the Superintendant of police to insist upon private residents to also effectually screen all lights.'

17 September 1915. A military dance took place in the Town Hall, when a large number of the soldiers stationed in the town and ladies of the town and district attended, and a jolly evening resulted. The MCs were Sgt Andrews and Cpl Wells and Transport Driver March. The music was supplied by the Melton Constable band under the direction of bandmaster Reed.

23 September 1915. The Harvest Thanksgiving Service attracted a large congregation, the church being crowded far beyond its ordinary seating capacity. The church had been tastefully and appropriately decorated. The special preacher was Canon Woosman, chaplain to the South Wales Mounted Brigade. The offerings of money amounted to £5 1s 4d were given to the Norfolk and Norwich Hospital, and the fruit and vegetables were sent to the Kelling Sanatorium.

24 September 1915. A heifer belonging to Mr JK Gooch fell down a dry well on his farm, a drop of some fifty feet. On being hauled up again with considerable difficulty by Mr Gooch, assisted by a trooper from the Montgomeryshire Yeomanry, was found to be little worse for the fall. There was a thick bed of decayed vegetation at the bottom of the shaft, and this undoubtedly broke the force of the fall.

10 October 1915. During the morning service at the parish church, the Rector, the Revd HA

e Reid family enjoys an outing
h the military on the Lowes.

King unveiled and dedicated a handsome stained glass window, erected in memory of two former members of the choir, Charles Henry Steer, Scots Guards, and Oliver Bennett (R.F.A.), both of whom have given their lives for their country. The Rector alluded in touching terms to these two old members and also of Charles Edward Dack (Norfolks) who lost his life last week. The choir sang Goss's anthem 'I heard a voice', and appropriate hymns were rendered.

13 October 1915. The celebrated Glamorgan Yeomanry Welsh Voice Choir visited Holt and gave two concerts in the Town Hall, which was kindly lent by Mr CW Jex, who in addition spared no efforts to make the visit of the celebrated choir a success. There were two splendid attendances. At night the place was packed, and scores of people stayed in the street opposite the hall unable to obtain admission. The concert was in aid of the funds of the Holt Literary Institute and the Yeomanry Fund for the Welsh wounded. So much has been written of the super-excellence of the choir, that it would be an invidious task to attempt to add to the glowing encomiums so lavishly and deservedly bestowed upon them. The part-singing was very fine indeed, and reflected great credit on their conductor Mr Frank Hill, FRCO (Aylsham).

21 October 1915. 'Our Day' at Holt was confined to the selling of flags in the streets and places of public resort by numerous persistent and importunate ladies, under the superintendence of Mrs Meyrick Jones and Mrs RT Hales. Starting at an early hour, they had quickly exhausted the original supply of bags and a further two thousand were sent for, and these too were readily disposed of. It was a rare sight to see anyone not wearing a flag. Indeed, in one well-known establishment in town, one of the young men had at least twenty flags of all shapes and sizes pinned to him and besides this Lothario, there were others whose adornment showed an inability to deny the importunities of the lady collectors, and whose pockets must have been sadly depleted at the end of the day.

27 October 1915. The death in France of 2nd Lieut. WW Ireland of the 2nd Royal Sussex was officially notified. Lieut. Ireland was known better to the great majority of the townsfolk Regimental Sgt. Major Ireland, for it was in that capacity he came to the town with the Sixth Sussex. He was of the very best type of English non-commissioned officer, and by his geniality and his many sterling qualities as a soldier and as a man he made a host of friends in the town. His death at an early age will be regretted by all who had the privilege of knowing him.

11 November 1915. A successful entertainment in aid of the British Red Cross Society took place in the Shirehall. Miss Eva Preston was responsible for the programme, and she was fortunate enough to enlist the services of some musical soldiers, with the result that a programme both lengthy and meritorious was presented. The Shirehall was well filled with an appreciative audience, who plainly enjoyed the excellent fare put before them.

20 November 1915. The death occurred at his residence in Mulbarton of Mr Robert William Daplyn, who for many years kept the Feathers Hotel, and who through his kindness and affability made a host of friends in the town. At the funeral which took place on the 26th, some of Mr Daplyn's old Holt friends were present, and a beautiful floral tribute inscribed 'From old friends at Holt' was placed on the coffin.

FEATHERS HOTEL

Mr RW Daplyn, towards the end of his life.

Russell Hunt

We first met Russell Hunt at the printing-works of Rounce and Wortley, where he had been apprenticed to the trade. He features in this photo (right) of the Preston family and their apprentices in front of the Reliance Printing Works in the High Street, probably taken prior to 1908. For a few months of his time as a soldier, Russell kept a diary, to which we have been given access. This is the first time it has been in the public domain.

Everything happened to Russell except being killed; he volunteered in high spirits, he underwent training full of anticipation of glorious deeds ahead, he went out to France, he fought on the Somme, he endured atrocious conditions in the trenches, he was wounded, he lost comrades, he was captured and a Prisoner of War for months, if not years. In using these extracts from his diary, I see him respresenting all Holt men who went to war and fought for their country. Some, like Russell, returned, and their war workhas been forgotten. Others did not return, and their name is inscribed in stone, for ever, on a memorial in the Market Place, where the traffic roars on by.

Except, of course, we are now remembering Russell and his experiences, through an improbable sequence of little events. He wrote his diary in pencil, in snatched moments between acts of war. This small, vulnerable book came through all his time in uniform, through all his trials and wounds, to lie unknown in a secret place in his home for the next seventy years. He never spoke of it, did not leave instructions about it, and probably, even, forgot it. On his death, his daughter Mary Butcher came across it for the first time. She passed it to the Regimental Museum, where it was transcribed – a copy of which was lent to me. We start with his decision to write.

Russell Hunt, on the right, is standing in front of the printing works of Arthur Preston where he was an apprentice, together with George Andrew Dady and William John Coke. On the left are Thomas, Sidney and Chamberlain Preston with their father in the doorway.

May 9 1915. My estimable friend and colleague William Jefferies and myself have from this day decided to keep a diary relating our various experiences in His Majesty's Army.

October 1 1914. I observe that my King and Country need me and forthwith make arrangements with my employer to enlist tomorrow.

Russell spent a month outside Folkestone for preliminary training before travelling to Colchester where he spent seven months 'good hard work'.

He clearly impressed his superiors with this attitude, and notes:

April 7 1915. For some inconceivable reason they saw fit to make me a Lance-Corporal. Likewise Billy.

He now settles at a camp at Codford.

May 1 1915. We are in huts. Mine is appropriately called the Dodger's Den.

May 18 1915. This evening, while taking a stroll over the hills, Billy and I discussed our chance of living through the war, but of course life is so uncertain that we abandoned the discussion.

Russell's diary includes many details of his military training, all fascinating, but too lengthy for inclusion here. What I have tried to do in making these selections is to portray, through his own words, his own passage as a Norfolk man at war. Russell does not seem to have distinguished himself with his rifle practice, but showed promise in observation work.

June 3 1915. I have handed in my rifle and bayonet, entrenching tool etc, owing to being Company Range-taker. I shall probably have a pistol for protection at the front.

He returns to Norfolk for a weekend of leave, aware that he will not be back before seeing action in France. Back in camp, a general edginess prevails. It is time to settle debts with his Holt employer.

July 8 1915. Much the same work as yesterday, with the exception that I dodged it on the plea that I was waiting to parade for teeth extraction, which did not come off. We are informed by tonight's that we are to commence mobilisation Thursday next. Our time in England is apparently getting very short. I forwarded ten shillings ten pence to Mr Wortley yesterday in payment of the watch I had previously purchased.

They expect the order to France at any minute.

July 14 1915. A memorable day owing to the fact that we commence mobilisation. We have drawn new putties.

July 16 1915. There should have been a Brigade Route March, but it was cancelled owing to rain. I lost a good deal on cards in consequence. I drew a fine pair of Field Glasses today for my Observing work.

July 21 1915. Busy today in mobilisation work. There was a general inspection which I did not attend. I practised revolver shooting in the miniature range using Lt Grand's revolver. I did fairly well for the first time. I have since drawn my own revolver, a genuine Colt automatic. What lies in the future?

And so they make the long-awaited journey to France. It proved to be stop and start all the way.

July 27 1915. Up early this morning and entrained at Boulogne station. Passed no end of village stations, finally disentrained at Berton. Loudly acclaimed by the peasants of various places. Marched about eight miles and billeted at Meter-de-Bois in a fairly comfortable house. Purchased an egg from the farmer for supper. Am doing well in picking up the French language. Germans have been here.

Russell is now in France; there is a period of just over a fortnight, spent in various locations

behind the front line, before his introduction to the trenches. He is wide-eyed and alert, excited to be in a new country, apprehensive about what may lie ahead, but keen to record all his impressions. There is a growing ease in his written style, direct, with an economical use of language. There is a lot of marching to be done with heavy packs. He enjoys the opportunity to describe what he sees. At times he begins to question some of the army routines to which they all have to submit. A sense of irony is born. With the space available for the diary in this volume, I can only quote a bare few of his entries.

Our rations chiefly consist of corned beef and biscuits.... The boys had a high night, owing to having been paid previously... 'C' company confined to barracks as a result of the ver du vie.... suffering from chronic internal pains... was disturbed in my slumbers by rats... I had a delightful bathe in a large pond just outside Avelay before returning to billet.... Received another letter from Salisbury... We are expecting to go into the trenches on Sunday... Lost a considerable sum at pontoon.

The entry for August 7th must stand for many of the others.

August 7 1915. Parade at 12.10 for trench-digging one and a half miles from the Firing Line. It rained when we started and we wore our waterproof sheets. En route we passed through the fine town of Albert,

EIGHT SONS SERVING.
IS THIS A NORFOLK RECORD?

The eight Soldier Sons of Mr. and Mrs. H. Cooke, of Peacock-lane, Holt. A ninth son will be joining up shortly.
1—Pte. H. R. Cooke, 3rd Norfolks.
2—Driver J. L. Cooke, R.F.A., Salonika.
3—Pte. H. E. Cooke, Royal Fusiliers.
4—Driver F. A. Cooke, A.S.C., France.
5—W. S. Cooke, R.N.A.S.
6—Rf. C. Cooke, P.O. Rifles, France.
7—Sergt. A. S. Cooke, Royal Irish Regt. Wounded and taken prisoner at the Battle of Mons. The photo has been sent from Germany.
8—Pte. B. S. Cooke, 3rd Essex.

PRELIMINARY NOTICE.

THE GREAT WAR FILM,

"BATTLE OF THE SOMME"

WILL BE SCREENED AT

The ELECTRIC PAVILION, HOLT,

ON MONDAY, DECEMBER 4th, and during the week.

which is now one mass of ruins. Large factories and buildings shelled to the ground. The very fine church looked a picture of debris. The town, once flourishing, is uninhabited. From information received, the Germans were driven out of this place by the French last December. We passed through the village of Aveloy, on the far side of which we dug our trenches. Our work for the day was accomplished without incident, except for a few

Russell Hunt

shells going overhead, one of which dropped in Albert, as if to remind it that it was not out of danger.

An uncomfortable jauntiness follows his first day in action.

August 16 1915. Our first day in the trenches proved interesting. I discovered that the German trenches were 350 yards away and I took the first opportunity of notifying them of my arrival, which compliment was speedily returned.

When posting the sentry on the listening post at night, I distinctly heard a working-party of the Germans digging in front of their trenches. This was reported to our officer and very shortly afterwards our artillery obliged the Germans with a few iron rations. Very little noise was heard after that.

Russell is progressively exposed to the realities of warfare, and the language he uses in his diary becomes more immediate. For reasons of space, I make brief selections only here.

I had rather a narrow escape this tea-time, a German shell dropping to within eight yards of where I was standing, fortunately only the earth hit me... received a card from Dad and a letter from Maud... at 5.15 pm we moved further up the line where dug-outs were conspicuous by their absence, and we consequently had to stand up all night. I could get no sleep whatsoever... I regret to announce our first casualty, a young fellow of No. 9 platoon was shot in the head and seriously wounded... I witnessed a German aeroplane being shelled by our guns but without success... I believe this is the river Somme. The place is almost deserted of civilians and assumes rather a squalid appearance, otherwise surrounded by very pretty country... we have a new Officer now, a Mr Spencer, I believe rather a decent fellow... the Germans started shelling us with shrapnel, two fellows were seriously wounded. It was four hours before we were able to get out, as we were unable to move the wounded men. It was an awful time as we were like rats in a cage and shells were falling all over the place. This is the worst time we have yet experienced. ...received a parcel of stationery from Mr Wortley, also 100 cigarettes. Letters from Maud and Daisy.

Things were to get worse for Russell. He was ordered to man a listening post called the 'Blood Pit' – 'a post within 12 yards of the German lines and most difficult to get to. Seven men are reported to have been killed here.' Day after day he has to man this post, contending with vermin at his feet and German shells all about. Moreover, 'a German officer is reported to have been seen in our lines.'

We now approach a critical episode in Russell's war.

Now I have to relate a very sad, though exciting, story, an experience which I shall never forget, and I trust never experience again.' His own officer, the much-liked Mr Spencer, had a even more daunting mission for him. He planned to lead a small party of Russell and two other men to check out a small wood which lay between the Blood Pit and the enemy lines. It was believed enemy snipers were concealed here. And so he begins. 'We traversed halfway up 'Blood Alley', where we mounted the parapet, and the four of us crawled on our hands and knees in file. We crawled along for about ten minutes when our Officer started out on a different track. The result of this was that we were all separated.' Russell crept up a furrow which ran parallel to the trench, but then lay low, awaiting developments, fearing the noise of snapping twigs would announce his whereabouts. He heard several shots, but stayed where he was. A minute later, his two comrades approached, aiming rifles at him in their confusion. At this point Russell's narrative becomes somewhat obscure; it is clear that Mr Spencer has been badly wounded. They all return to base, a search party of volunteers set out, find Spencer, and return with him. 'The poor fellow was shot through the arm and in the back of his head, the bullet grazing his back as it passed through; one day I may give this tale in detail. I will say no more now.

It is very clear from the writing that this experience had profound effect on Russell. But back to the trenches it was, with a vengeance. There follow more snatched excerpts, like gunfire…

'Duty at 'Blood Pit', 12noon to 6pm. Back to the scene of the crime. Sniper is still busy… the artillery are also shelling quite close to my post, some shrapnel is dropping in… relieved at 6pm by Lancs Fusiliers… had not been out of there more than half an hour when the Germans started to shell our trenches heavily. One huge shell fell near the 'Blood Pit', thankful to be out of it…

News of a temporary respite

I have just heard the glad news we are going out tomorrow night… Slept most of the day… Sunday, voluntary church parade for which I did not volunteer… Had some cigarettes come from my late landlady in Holt.

But it proved to be a short reprieve only.

The Germans are sending sausages over every few minutes. These are awful sausage-shaped bombs which make a terrific report and cause a great deal of damage… Received a letter from Dad and Maud… should have a day off, but was put in charge of twelve men for fatigue, morning and afternoon, filling sand-bags and repairing parapet. Shifted into support after tea, during which the Germans sent half a dozen sausages over, causing us to scatter in all directions. It is very fortunate that these sausages can be detected coming or we should have suffered many casualties ere this… A glorious morning and one feels glad to be alive despite being in the trenches… Wrote to Mother and Dad, also to Maud… I regret to state that Cpl Myles was killed this afternoon by an explosive bullet. He was a very nice fellow and the loss will be mourned by many… After tea we moved into the place where 'D' Company had previously been. This is a veritable death trap and consists of no less than six listening posts, all of which are no more than a few feet from the German parapet… In the early morning the enemy started sending some of their terrible sausages over, to which our howitzer battery replied. Then commenced a regular firing of shells, sausages, hand grenades and bombs. Pieces of shell etc were flying all around us. I made myself as small as possible, and fortunately we all escaped being hit… I expect I shall be on that beastly post again tonight. I received a parcel from Mother this morning, containing the usual luxuries, also a pipe and some shaving material. I have just read the joyful news that we are going out tomorrow morning. Oh, hasten the hour.

Russell was granted home leave in early December. After his return to the front, he found he could not resume his daily writing habit. ' I have been fed up ever since I came back from home, and have neglected to enter everything into my diary. Perhaps all the better.' My interpretation of this would be that he found the contrast between his two worlds – that of home, that of fighting, just too great. He managed to write about a week in February 1916, he recorded his promotion to Corporal on June 8th 1916, and continued until receiving a bad leg wound on June 30th, after which he returned to England for hospital treatment. His last entry for July 8th reads 'Different dressing on wound.'

Although there are no further diary entries, we know from his family that he returned to his regiment in France, and resumed life on the front line. In the course of an attack, he was captured by the Germans and held prisoner for a considerable time. He eventually escaped with a friend, and though his weight was down to seven stone, he walked towards the English lines.They encountered a number of German troops, who, to their great surprise, walked on by. It was then they realised the war was over.

Russell spent some time in English hospitals, but made a good recovery. He returned to his job with Rounce and Wortley, and in due course married Audrey, the daughter of Walter Horne, stone mason, Obelisk Plain.

Letheringsett Glavenside

One of the significant local initiatives to help wounded servicemen got under way In Letheringsett, under the auspices of the Red Cross, at the instigation of Mrs Alice Hales. Jane Hales wrote:

> My mother organised a Red Cross detachment and got them trained in First Aid and home nursing. In 1916 Mr Sidney Cozens-Hardy lent his Letheringsett home, 'Glavenside' as an auxiliary hospital for the sick and wounded. The patients wore light blue flannel suits, with white shirts and red ties, for most of them were convalescent. There were twenty-two beds, and the hospital was run entirely by volunteers, with the exception of two trained nurses, one of whom was Matron. My mother was Commandant and she went the mile to Letheringsett in the pony cart.

The hospital first opened on December 9th 1915 and continued its operation until early in January 1919. Records of its work are extant, and reveal a high take-up of beds. On average, 18.7 beds were in use, of the twenty-two available. In all, 386 patients were treated in the lifetime of the hospital.

A certificate of commendation to Alice Hales for her work at Glavenside.

Holt Peace Celebrations, July 19, 1919

Dallas Wynne Wilson gave a speech during Holt Peace Celebrations. His concluding words were "Today is a day of Thanksgiving for the end of the most tremendous five years of human history, of gratitude to those who have won the end, of hope for the future. For five years the Nation – the World – has been in the throes of

fever and delirium. Now it is convalescent and like convalescents it is somewhat fractious and peevish. But nurses tell us that such symptoms are signs of returning health. Still, we shall not be wholly recovered till these symptoms disappear. All can help. Let none of us throw away the patience, the brotherliness, the sanity, the unselfishness that drew the nation together till victory. Demobilise everything else but not that."

The War Memorial

Names of Holt men, inscribed on the War Memorial, who died in the First World War

ANTHONY Alfred. Died on 27th November 1919

BENNETT Oliver. Killed in action in France & Flanders on 21st October 1914.

BERESFORD Robert. Died in Gallipoli on 21st August 1915.

BETTS William. Died on 20th February 1916.

BOAST Thomas. No further information available at present.

BRAY Albert. Died of wounds at home on 10th February 1917.

BRAY Charles. Killed in action in France & Flanders on 16th August 1917.

BULLOCK Horace. Killed in action in France & Flanders on 6th September 1918.

CASTON Albert. Killed in action in France & Flanders on 15th September 1916.

CASTON Alfred. Died in France & Flanders on 29th July 1918.

CHESTNEY Frederick. Died in France & Flanders on 9th December 1917.

CLARKE Charles. Killed in action in France & Flanders on 13th October 1915.

COCKADAY Albert. Killed in action in Palestine on 19th April 1917.

COOPER Ernest. Killed in action in France & Flanders on 29th August, 1918.

COTTS Fred. Died on 14th May 1919.

COTTS Thomas. Killed in action in France & Flanders on 17th May 1915.

DACK Charles. Killed in action in France & Flanders on 30th September 1915.

DACK Ernest. Killed in action with the British Expeditionary Force on 28th September 1916.

DACK Sidney. Died of wounds in France & Flanders on 26th August 1916.

DIX William. Killed in action in France & Flanders on 9th May 1915.

DIXON Joseph. No further information available at present

FLOOD George. Killed in action in France & Flanders on 6th April 1915.

GRAVELING James. Killed in action in France & Flanders on 31st August 1918.

GREENGRASS Edward. No further information available at present

GROUT Frederick. Killed in action in France & Flanders on 8th February 1916.

GUYMER Ernest. No further information available at present

HERRON Fred. No further information available at present

HORNE Reginald. Son of Walter Horne, Obelisk Plain

HOUCHEN William. Killed in action in France & Flanders on 20th October 1917.

JENKINSON Herbert. Died of wounds in France & Flanders on 29th August 1917.

KNIGHTS Richard. Died on 22nd August 1920.

KNOWLES John. Died of wounds in France & Flanders on 1st November 1915.

LAKE Benjamin. No further information available at present.

LEWIS Victor. Killed in action in France & Flanders on 14th July 1916.

LOADES Charlie. Died of wounds in France & Flanders on 7th September 1918.

LOYNES Robert. Killed in action in France & Flanders on 6th June 1918.

MANN Walter. Killed in action in France & Flanders on 15th March 1917.

MAYES Victor. Killed in action in France & Flanders on 13th April 1916.

McMAHON Joseph. Died of wounds in France & Flanders on 4th October 1917.

MEARS Frank. Killed in action in France & Flanders on 10th April 1918.

MIDDLETON William. Killed in action in France & Flanders on 3rd May 1917.

MURRELL Lewis. Killed in action in France & Flanders on 24th April 1918.

142

MURRELL Wallace. Died in Gallipoli on 21st August 1915. Aged 25.

NEAL Archer. (Military Medal). Killed in action in France & Flanders on 15th September 1916.

NEAL William. Died of wounds in France & Flanders on 4th July 1916.

NEAL William. Killed in action in France & Flanders on 27th September 1917.

NICHOLS Robert. Died of wounds in France & Flanders on 13th March 1915.

NICHOLS William. Killed in action in France & Flanders on 29th September 1918.

PELLS William. Killed in action in France & Flanders on 26th August 1916.

POINTER Herbert. Died in France & Flanders on 28th February 1917.

PRESTON Sidney. (son of Arthur Preston) No other information available.

RICHES Edward. Died of wounds in France & Flanders on 5th August 1917.

RUDD Horace. Killed in action in France & Flanders on 19th July 1916.

SHARPIN Harry. Killed in action in France & Flanders on 9th July 1915.

SMITH William. Killed in action in France & Flanders on 21st March 1918.

SMITH Vivian, Captain. Killed in action on 13th November 1916.

STARLING James. Killed in action in France & Flanders on 28th April 1917).

STEER Charles. Killed in action in France & Flanders on 26th October 1914.

WAKEFIELD Albert. No further information available at present.

WALLER Firmage. Died of wounds in France & Flanders on 28th March 1918.

WALLER Albert. Killed in action in France & Flanders on 4th October 1917.

WATSON Geoffrey. Died of wounds in France & Flanders on 4th August 1918.

WHITE Robert. Died in Mesopotamia on 14th July 1918.

British Legion

The British Legion became a very strong force in Holt in the 20s and 30s.

Earle Kirby My father was a former soldier so he joined the British Legion, he was an excellent book-keeper so he became secretary, and then they found out that he could play the trumpet, because he'd played the bugle in the army. They asked him to play the Last Post on Armistice Day, so he went behind the yard behind Robinson's garage, and he played the Last Post so beautifully, that brought everybody into tears, and from then on, my father could do no wrong in Holt. He was accepted.

BRITISH — LEGION.

Holt and District Branch Committee, 1926-27.

ck row, left to right: S Moulton, R Harmer, LW Clark, G Jarrold, √ Bond, H Lee, AG Wright, H Sergeant, T Nicholls, R Lee.

nt row: BH Bond, CW Jex, GD Hayden, HW Moulton, AE Coe, Weston, G Wasey.

ST. ANDREW'S

CHURCH STREET

Library

Church
Hall

OLD SCHOOL HOUSE

HEMPSTEAD ROAD

MARKET
PLACE

CHAPTER
SEVEN

Chapter 7

Revd E Brumell

The Reverend E Brumell
(Rector of Holt, 1853–1901)

Jane Hales gives a delightful portrait of Holt's Rector, who just qualifies for the twentieth century!

The Rector's daily routine, according to hearsay, began with a cold bath. After breakfast, he walked up the hill, through the town and round the Lowes. On his way back he stopped at the National School to give a lesson. He also took out the children at night, on to the Spout Hills, to teach them the rudiments of astronomy. He was rich, and put in new and uncomfortable pews into the nave of the church. The orderly years rolled by. Edward Brumell's wife died and his niece came to keep house. For the first twenty-nine years of his incumbency, there was no organ in the church, and the mixed choir sang with the aid of a tuning-fork. As he grew older, the Rector read the services slower and slower; honey dropped on to the pews, as there were bees in the plain, eighteenth century roof. After it was all over, old women curtsied to the Rector, and he gave them half-crowns. The more artful hurried up the Bull Street, and caught him again on his way through the town (if not driven off by the Churchwardens) and the forgetful old man would give out more coins. The Parson was a teetotaller, but he was no spoilsport, and there was good wine for his guests. He himself liked sweet food, and would disorganise the Victorian dinner party by asking for another syllabub after the dish had been removed from the room.

Funeral procession of the Revd E Brumell in 1901.

The successor to the Revd E Brumell was the Revd Lewis B Radford, DD, who is best remembered by his book, History of Holt, a brief study of Church, Parish and School. He was rector between 1902 and 1908. The book's sub-title shows his main area of interest; his text is clear and elegant, and his research authoritative – essential for our knowledge of earlier history.

List of chapters

Holt from the Ninth to the Thirteenth Century
Priests and Parishioners of Holt
The Parish Church of St Andrew, 1340–1540
Holt during the Reformation
Holt from the Civil War to the Revolution
Holt under the Georges, 1782–1820
Holt in the Nineteenth Century
Gresham's School, Holt

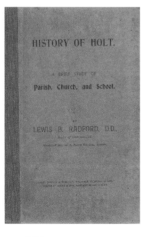

He ends his chapter on the nineteenth century in Holt, (over half of whose nine pages concern the fabric of the church),

v of interior before
oval of gallery, 1907.

with a swift look at other matters. This leads him to a general review of social changes over the previous hundred years, looking back to 1808. As we are now embarked on a similar span of enquiry with regard to Holt, it is interesting to read the last few sentences of this chapter, through which we may understand the writer's prevailing frame of reference. He's been talking of Holt's horse-borne access to the wider world.

Things have changed since those days. Corridor trains and liners, telegraph and parcel post, parish councils and boards of education – the whole machinery of life and work has passed through a rapid evolution which has left the year 1808 centuries behind. Man himself, has changed, too, on the surface in many things, deeper down in not a few. Behind him lies the experience of his fathers; it is at once his privilege and responsibility to read the lessons of that experience. They may be read in the story of the parish as in the story of the nation, for the parish is a nation in miniature; and the key to either story is the conviction that while again and again 'The old order changeth, yielding place to new', it is only because God fulfils Himself in many ways.

Some years after leaving Holt, his former parishioners hear of his progress in Australia.

Holt Almanack 1916. The many friends in Holt and district of Dr LB Radford, who was rector of the parish from 1902 to 1908, will be gratified to hear of his appointment as Bishop of Goulburn, in New South Wales. When Rector of Holt, Dr Radford was known, far beyond the confines of the parish and diocese for his many activities in varying spheres, and even at that time his many friends regarded high preferment for him as most probable. He went out to Sydney as Master of St Paul's Hostel at Sydney University, taking up his work in the early part of 1909. Now, after six years work in Australia, further preferment has been accorded him.

riage solemnised at
ndrew's on 19th April
6, between Nelly Mendall
er and Horace Allen
:e, both of Holt. The
e's father is listed as
< butcher, and the
om's as coachbuilder.

Radford identifies the following changes to the church building in the early years of the century.

'St Andrew's – building changes

The Resurrection window in the south aisle was given in 1905 by John Rogers, Esq. of Holt Hall, in memory of his wife Mary Palmer Rogers; the window representing St John, St Peter and St Andrew was given in 1905 by Sir Alfred Jodrell in memory of the late rector, the Revd E Brumell. Both are the work of Bryans, a pupil of Kempe. In 1907 a faculty was obtained for a general scheme of restoration, and towards this scheme the sum of £1,000 was raised within the year, of which £500 was given by JH Burcham-Rogers, Esq. and £100 by Miss Rogers. The tower was completely restored, and a turret built to carry the belfry stairs, and the two bells re-hung in a new four-bell frame at an entire cost of £800. The next step was the removal of the north gallery; it remains now to restore the roof and walls of the nave and aisles throughout, and to build a new vestry or enlarge the old.'

The Reverend HA King

The Revd HA King at his desk.

Dora Hills gave this overall verdict on the Holt of her childhood: The Revd King and Mrs King were the backbone of Holt.

The living of St Andrew's is the gift of St John's College, Cambridge, and fell vacant when Dr Radford became Warden of St Paul's College, Sydney. It was customary to appoint a Johnian, if available, to the charge, and Herbert King proved the ideal choice. He had already spent sixteen years as curate in London until the age of thirty-seven, so was experienced in parish work, had a young family, and was keen to take responsibility of a parish of his own. His son John notes that there must have been several compelling reasons for his parents to move to Holt. Apart from the evident attractions of the house and garden, there was the re-founded Gresham's to take into account: 'Since 1900, owing to the wisdom and inspiration of the Fishmongers Company, Sir John Gresham's Grammar School had been developed and elevated into the status of Public School of a most unusual type, appealing strongly to liberal-minded, intelligent and artistic parents who saw undesirable elements in traditional public schools.' Another small consideration was the stipend on offer at Holt – £680 per annum – a 'handsome' figure, according to son John. Particularly so, as the salary on which he was living as a curate was £180. He took the job, and the family moved to Holt early in 1909.

So began his work as parish priest, which he continued for almost forty years – until his death, in fact, in 1947. From the outset, he gave himself utterly to the role he had chosen, not only specifically in connection with the church, but with a whole range of other town activities. His wife, equally, made a strong contribution, especially with Brownies and Guides. As a pair, they operated, in an era, and in a size of parish, in which they could become the very epitome of the clerical couple; and with their large family, they won the hearts of their parishioners.

Sunday in Church

The Revd King's daughter Beatrice recalls the Sunday routine.

el Potter "In church on
days I used to sit with
mum in front of
dener Cotts. It would be
ing to the end of the
n and Cotts would be
ing his Amen well after
ryone else. It was so loud
I was fascinated. I would
round and gaze in
der at the big man and
noisy Amen. Mum would
me round quickly, but I
ld often see Cotts' wife
ing a little smile."

On Sunday we always wore special Sunday clothes. The day started with learning the catechism, and later the Collect for that particular Sunday. Some I can still remember by heart. Off we went to church, walking, of course, and through the lovely, sweet-smelling avenue of limes to St. Andrew's Church. Sailor suits and hats for both boys and girls were the order of the day and no doubt passed down from the older to the younger children. Boater hats for both, but pleated skirts for the girls and trousers for the boys. Later, we girls wore pretty frocks and big hats decorated with flowers, wearing gloves and carrying prayer books and purses with our penny for the collection.

otism card of Doreen
rahams (nee Cubitt Cooke).
ster Day, 16th April 1922

We always sat at the back of the church; we thought my mother did not like to be inspected from behind, or it may have been a wise precaution in case we behaved badly. Later, when servants were scarce or non-existent, we thought she liked to slip away quickly to see how the joint was doing; and one can't blame her for that as the rectory was quite a long walk away. Can one ever forget dear old Amy Skrimshire, our doctor's sister, who hooted rather than sang the hymns, and who always finished the line when we were almost halfway on to the next line. She was blind, so she had to memorise the words.

One or two other episodes come to mind: Dorothea, who during a christening, piped in a very loud voice with the remark that our father was washing the baby's hair.

las Wynne Wilson There
s a curate in those days at
t who certainly caused us
ne amusement. He was
y short, and when I first
v him in the pulpit only
head and shoulders were
ble; but suddenly he shot
to an astonishing height
ving mounted on top of
kneeler. His sermon
jan in rather startling
hion: 'My friends:–
tius Pilate was a cad.'

Then I shall always remember our beloved Auntie Hilda, pseudo aunt, who loved singing 'Ye watchers and ye holy ones', with all those alleluias. I can still see her with those rimless glasses looking down at me with a twinkle in her eye, with her little puckered mouth letting rip the alleluias! Auntie Hilda was rather a society lady, a friend of my mother's from Cheltenham College days. She seemed to enjoy our rather unconventional family.

Sometimes there was an occasional let-down from the organ. Air had to be pumped into it from behind, but now and again the village lad who was hired to do the pumping was dreaming or fast asleep and so no notes came from the organ. The choir had to carry on unaccompanied until the lad started pumping again. I used to pump for John who practised on the organ, and so I sat in the dark cubby hole. Of course, I did it for nothing, but I did enjoy doing it!

149

The Choir

Here is a photo of St Andrew's choir, 1910 – only a year into the Revd King's incumbency, so we may assume he inherited a strong tradition from his predecessor. Francis now gives a wonderful account of its character and quality:

Men, starting from the left:
Frank Smith, Mr Kaberry,
Mr Bush, Mr Dix, Dr Skrimshire,
Revd HA King, Geoffrey Shaw,
Bernard Craske, Tom Preston,
Mr W Smith.

Boys: E Bond, Sid Beresford,
Alec Beith, W Loades,
Fred Bush, C Cooke, E Dack,
W Back, G Cooke, W Bond,
R Firmage, A Cockaday,
B Bond, C Pearce

A word should now be said about the Holt choir. John and I were members of the church choir in its heyday, and there had been a quite a well-balanced, large choir for many years. There is a photograph of it ranged up, standing in the midst of no less a person than Geoffrey Shaw who must have been the choirmaster at the time, I imagine, to warrant his inclusion. He with his brother Martin Shaw along with Vaughan Williams and Percy Dearmer had produced the English Hymnal. His influence must have made something of an impact. He was music master at Gresham's where he made such an impression on a visiting inspector that he was snatched away to be an inspector himself, eventually becoming Chief Inspector of Music to the Board of Education. He and his family gave delightful impromptu concerts in the holidays, a memorable one taking place one summer's day in the open air theatre of Gresham's School.

The choir was a set of varied characters. The choirmaster was a Mr Steadman, a man of impeccable taste and musical judgement, patient and good-tempered beyond belief with us all. Kaberry was the basso profundo, a solid man with beetling eyebrows and indigo moustache and an air of great dignity and importance. It was his undisputed right to hold on to the last note of anything and everything – just that amount longer than anyone else. Frank Smith was a bluff, strong-minded man, also a bass, who from time to time felt it necessary to march out of a choir practice and deprive the choir of his services, as a protest to being asked to sing 'hardy gardy toones'. These toones were most often some of the loveliest ever written – early mediaeval French. However, he always forgave the rector and choirmaster, and returned after a week or two. Underneath he was a most loyal man. One cannot mention

them all, but Dix was the principal tenor. His musical judgement was always sound and he unswervingly backed the 'hardy gardy'.

We had two outstandingly good trebles amongst the boys – Kenneth Peck and Lloyd George Olley. They had lovely voices and considerable idea of style in singing. Their time in the choir marked the apex of its achievement perhaps. One year at a festival of Norfolk choirs in Norwich cathedral Holt choir was chosen to lead all of them in. This was probably done in rotation; the choir must have thought it was on merit, as the next time round when we came not to head the procession, indignation abounded. It was a good experience this singing, though at times John and I had to stiffen our flagging enthusiasm by remembering it was our duty to 'support home industries'.

The highlight of the choir year was the choir supper which took place in the autumn. Our gigantic Victorian mahogany table, with every leaf in, stretched from one end of the dining-room to the other. It seated all the men of the choir and the choirmaster, John and myself. Special help had to be got in for cooking, serving and washing up. The gathering was a good-humoured mix of characters, all differences forgotten. No need to describe the Dickensian fare which was followed by speeches and much thanks for 'coupling my name with the 'toost''. After, in the drawing-room, people were induced to do their party pieces – usually after some persuasion and a decent show of reluctance.

Clifford Watts, chorister

Clifford Watts was one of the smiling faces lined up for the camera to mark the closing of the Board School (Chapter Three). Here he tells us about his busy Sundays.

Clifford Watts "I was in the choir, yes, of course I was. I was a leading boy in the choir with Canon King, and Steadman, the organist, who was a farmer from Glandford; eight leading boys used to go down to the choir at Glandford – we were paid ten bob a quarter. We used to get a halfpenny for every attendance at Holt; that meant practice on Friday night, then Sunday morning, and Sunday night. Every first Sunday of the month we had to be in Glandford at nine, for Holy Communion; we then used to get back for the Sunday School in Holt for half-past ten, followed by the service at eleven o'clock. Home for dinner or whatever. Then we'd be there at Crowe's for two o'clock for three o'clock at Glandford. They'd take us in their charabanc, horse and cart, anything they'd got! Come home, go for a walk somewhere – Cromer Road – then back to church at night.

fford Watts

And... I thoroughly enjoyed it, I still do, I love Songs of Praise. I joined the choir, perhaps, at the age of eleven, and as the older boys moved off, I moved up. I tell you what, I sang a solo when King George 5th had congestion of the lungs, and he went down to Bognor for convalescence, and that's when Bognor Regis got its Regis! The church was full of Legion, Scouts, Guides, everybody, and I had the honour of that. There were probably twenty-four of us, there were two rows of seats, each side. I was a choir boy for five or six years, and once I got in there, I enjoyed it! My book was number 21 and my cassock was Q. All the choir used to go to a Christmas party at Bayfield Hall, and that was a good'un – and at the end there was a big sack come round with presents, and they were all good presents too. They'd be from Sir Alfred Jodrell. He used to be at Glandford Church every Sunday, and he used to open the vestry door for you, and always had a little drip on the end of his nose. He was only a little old fella."

Church Lane

The lane leading off the Market Place to the churchyard has some old houses. Cottages were pulled down to make way for the Church Hall, the building of which was begun before the 1914–18 war, but was not entirely finished until afterwards. One wall remains of a building near the entrance to the churchyard, which was demolished near the end of the last century. At the Church House lived William Withers Junior, who was a notable authority on the planting of trees. The fine avenue of limes leading up to the church is probably about a century old, (Jane Hales, 1967).

Wansbeck House

The County Library

The building which currently houses the library was built for a totally different purpose. It always seemed rather unlikely to me that such grand accommodation had been provided for horses, however valuable – until I came across Jane Hales' information about Mr John Banks.

The present County Library was stabling for Wansbeck House, the premises of which extended up to the churchyard wall. At Wansbeck House lived John Banks, a surgeon in the first half of the nineteenth century. He put up a memorial stone to his horse in the churchyard wall. 'To dear Moggie, most faithful of quadrupeds etc.' Unfortunately, this stone was removed when the wall was repaired in Canon King's time, and has disappeared. (Jane Hales)

Anybody with such love for his horse when dead could well have erected a palace for it in its lifetime!

James Olley

The man most associated with the Library building is the legendary figure of James Olley, veteran of the Crimean War, and one of the six hundred who took part in the illustrious Charge of the Light Brigade. Later in life, James Olley became destitute, but was rescued from poverty when his earlier gallantry became known. He was set up in business here, to train horses for the local gentry. For a full account of this man's exploits, see the rich and fascinating book Salthouse, The Story of a Norfolk Village.

The Church Hall

Jane Hales gives us a summary of the central role of the Church Hall in the first decades of the twentieth century:

> The heyday of the Church Hall was at the beginning of this century, before the home attractions of radio and television. The erection of the Church Hall was the idea of the Revd HA King. His brother, an architect, bought a piece of land by Church Lane Holt, and designed the new hall. But before this could be used for its intended purpose, the 1914–18 war broke out. The hall was occupied by soldiers, whose nailed boots spoilt the floorboards, so that fresh ones had to be put in. When peace came, all and sundry used the Church Hall for dances, parties, meetings, badminton and so forth, and the 'Sunflowers' concert party delighted audiences with their shows. Parson King did good service to the parish in organising University Extension Lectures in the hall. Holt was said to be the smallest centre in England, and that of course before the adult classes under the auspices of local education authorities. The earnest-minded and others came to the Church Hall for talks on Japanese history, on Russian Literature and various subjects. If there was a 'magic lantern', some took the opportunity of snoozing in the darkness.

m the Holt Almanack, 1929.

uary 17th 1925. A cessful invitation dance s held at the Parish Hall, h the object of augmenting funds of the Holt Literary titute. The hall was corated by Miss Bond, and refreshment department s ably superintended by s Byford. Mr R Byford's hestra played throughout evening.

uary 22nd 1928. The fifth ual Christmas treat for the dren of Holt, organised by Holt United Football Club k place in the Church Hall, en 219 children did justice an appetising tea. After tea, nmunity singing, carols, ividual songs, and itations occupied the time, each child received a sent, an orange and a cker.

o days before delivery of manuscript to the nters, this photo was ered to us by Lynne Hurst, lector of postcards, many whose finds are on these ges. We made room! It ows St Andrew's Football b, 1912–1913 season.

The Head Master, the Revd Reginald Jolliffe Roberts is seen here seated in the centre with one of his sons on his lap. Mr Howell is the other master wearing a mortar board. 'Billy' Thorpe, the Usher, is standing to the right of Revd Roberts, with moustache and cap.

The Holt Free Grammar School of Sir John Gresham

Unless you are already familiar with Gresham's story, it is hard to appreciate the astonishing changes it underwent in the first ten years of the twentieth century. The choice of the year 1900 for the starting-point of this book is more than arithmetically convenient, for it enables us to look at both 'versions' of Holt's famous school. Up to 1900, ever since its original foundation by Sir John Gresham in 1555, its full title had been The Holt Free Grammar School of Sir John Gresham. As from 1900, it changed absolutely in nature, scale, reputation and national influence, under its more simple name, Gresham's. Before that watershed date, it had been a small institution (around fifty scholars in 1900), serving town boys and those from slightly further afield in North Norfolk. After that date, it opened its doors to boys from throughout the land, and soon, overseas. In ten years, it

nding immediately
ind Mr Howell is a boy
h a small cap perched on
of his head. This is Harry
imshire, later to be doctor
e town. One other boy
can identify with
ainty is Bertie Ellis. He is
ted behind the boy with
s outstretched in front,
t to the right of this
tion. His cap is tipped
k on his head, he has a
ge, and his jacket is
ker than most.

moved from its cramped home in the town Market Place, to luxury accommodation down the Cromer Road. Numbers swelled to about two hundred in ten years. This newly-wrought Public School was the talk of the land. How?

Howson, Headmaster, 1900–1919, that's how! But we jump ahead. Let's first look at the school in the premises in the middle of town, which had been its home since the beginning, although totally rebuilt just forty or so years before, in 1858. Always under the patronage of the Fishmongers' Company, the school had, over the centuries, seen both lean and fat years. Since 1867, the Headmaster had been the Revd Reginald Jolliffe Roberts, a Classical scholar, assisted by Second Master, Mr Howell, and 'Billy' Thorpe, Usher. Fortunately, a pupil who spanned the changeover years, Canon Frederic Jarvis, wrote down his memories of tuition, at the eastern end of the Market Place, in the Grammar School era.

Grammar School Era.

OLD SCHOOL HOUSE.

Frederic Jarvis "The Revd Reginald Jolliffe Roberts, commonly called 'Bobbie', the last headmaster under the old régime, was tall, portly and whiskered. He presided over the big schoolroom, which was the large room at the north end of the building now known as the Old School House, and facing him the seniors sat in fours at long desks doing work on slates, which from time to time they would clean at the bowls of water which stood on the two 'tortoise' stoves by which the room was heated. He wielded the cane rarely and temperately, and was a kindlier man than the blue-eyed, beetle-browed, waxed moustached second master, Mr Howell of Wansbeck House, whose desk stood halfway down the room and immediately behind the seniors, from which he would emerge with silent swiftness and wildly thrash the neck and shoulders of some unfortunate boy caught talking. The other end of the room was occupied by the juniors under 'Billy' Thorpe, the Usher, who apparently had never heard of discipline or self-discipline, but with whose unruly class nobody attempted to interfere. In the small room adjoining, 'Froggie', as all French masters seem then to have been called, must have spent countless hours of misery trying to contend with impossible pupils. There was always much noise in the big schoolroom as those classes not working on slates at desks, sat on backless benches round three sides of the masters' desks, where they received instruction in Latin, History, Geography and the Catechism.

This picture of an educational establishment which, judged by modern standards looks depressing, had many good points, for though the methods and conditions were antiquated, a good grounding was given in all these subjects as well as in Mathematics. Furthermore, hard work was demanded, and boys were taught to read, write and spell better than they are today.

George Howson,
prospective Head Master

It must have seemed a depressing picture to the short, stoutish man who stepped into it during school hours one day, dressed in frock coat and silk hat, on a visit of inspection, but whose mind probably envisaged the new buildings which were shortly begin to rise from the ground on the Cromer Road and the new school he was to create out of the remnants of the old.

'Bobbie' Roberts finished up with five boarders, of which I was one. We lived in fear of his fearsome wife, and his kind and gentle daughter Ethel lived in fear of us. Of these five I was the only one who remained to be one of the seven boarders with whom Howson started, and to see the sweeping changes which took place, both in the house and in the school, where all the disadvantages had still to be contended with.

New classrooms, known as the 'Tin Tab', were erected on the playing-field in which Eccles taught science at one end and Miller taught German at the other. In the house, one dormitory soon increased to four, and Eccles started a second house at Wansbeck. In the school, an iron discipline was at first enforced, but this gradually developed into what became known as Howson's system, and when this was established the cane was abolished.

All our hopes and expectations in those early days were set on the great change which was to come, and our Sunday walk was always to the new buildings to register what progress had been made. Late one night (the night before the move), the Headmaster invited the Captain of his house and two prefects to take up their bedding and go with him to be the first to sleep in the complete new School House which today is called by his name.

We will give the full background to this phenomenal transformation in Chapter Eight, when our journey takes us down the Cromer Road.

Dallas Wynne Wilson – Housemaster

As we have already seen, Dallas Wynne Wilson was housemaster at Old School House during the period of the First World War. But he started his career there much earlier, in 1905, when the premises were relinquished by the senior school. His memoirs make it plain that the accommodation was not particularly suitable for boarding purposes, and before long there was a major crisis.

> After a year or so a matron came to us who was perfectly invaluable, and she has been a close personal friend of ours ever since. She had enormous capacity for work, an excellent influence over the boys, and was one of the most conscientious and loyal people I have ever met. Her worth was well proved when after a couple of years we were faced with a real crisis. This was in the autumn term of 1907. The House had been 're-decorated' for us when we came in, but I don't think the gas system had been overhauled properly, and also we were taking more boys than the cubic space in each dormitory really allowed. In October of that year we began to be seriously alarmed by the number of boys with sore throats, and finally two of these developed diphtheria. The school doctor, Gillam, advised us, the headmaster and the governors, that we should evacuate the house for the present. We went over to Sheringham and found two houses available on the top of what is known as Hook's Hill, and thither we moved at two days' notice. We actually made the move itself, however, in just one day; forty boys slept in their beds at the Old School House in the morning and were sleeping in the same beds and bedding that same night at Sheringham.

Dallas Wynne Wilson There was a character in Holt known as Charlie who had been a member of the Salvation Army and still wore the uniform. He used to preach outside the Old School House during Preparation and insisted, when we remonstrated, that he must do the Lord's work. I am afraid we replied that he made it impossible for the boys to do theirs. He scarcely had any audience; but one evening I was in my bedroom at the Woods' house and heard a noise of falling water. I looked out, and there kneeling by the pump at the street corner was Charlie, praying loudly, and over him stood another man with a pail which he steadily filled with water from the pump and poured over Charlie. I think the poor man on the whole rather enjoyed this species of martyrdom. Later he was 'put away' as he talked too much about 'turning children into angels' – prematurely, of course!

He pays tribute to all the medical staff who attended his boys.

Doctors and Matrons have as much (and sometimes more) to do with the well-being of the school as the magisterial staff. We were most fortunate with our doctors: they were close and valued friends. Three of them we shall always especially remember: they all three died in harness. All Norfolk knew them. J B Gillam was our first doctor who helped us through our trouble with diphtheria and consequent move to Sheringham. I quote from the obituary notice in the school magazine: 'He had an unfailing kindness and courtesy, a rigid honesty of purpose, a shrewd knowledge of men and a rare sense of humour…all kinds of classes mourn for him as an intimate friend.' He died at the early age of forty-eight.

He has (mainly) fond memories of rather cramped games of cricket.

We were very well off at the Old School House for playing fields, as the field which had served the whole school for many generations and contained, I think, about twelve acres for cricket and football was now wholly at the disposal of my small boys. Till then all the boys of the school had played there, and I remember during that summer taking part in cricket there with five games going on, mid-on to one, long-leg to another, and deep-field at no very long range to two others. It was not a comfortable position but I never actually saw any accident. It is a lovely field, for it has a number of fine trees round it, including two or three magnificent walnuts.

However, the spectators to his bravura scoring strokes annoyed him exceedingly!

Even for one game of cricket the ground was small, and it was possible to hit out of it without much difficulty, anyhow for myself. It was bordered by a stone wall dividing it from the main road and this wall on half-holiday afternoons was lined with idlers from the village. They were inclined to 'barrack' me decidedly when I happened to get hold of a half volley from a small bowler and hit it over the wall. I often quoted to myself a verse from, I think, the book of Samuel or Kings: "My soul loatheth the men that sit upon the wall".

He now continues with an allusion to the sheer numbers of domestic staff required to run his establishment, an aspect of the school's operation to which we will return in our next chapter.

We engaged a strapping cook at the outset, a Danish woman, who had a lot of experience at some great London store, and

for a time she ruled the kitchen with a rod of iron and all was peace. But unfortunately after a year or two she had to go owing to excessive slaking of the thirst engendered by working in front of a range! We had eight or nine dormitory and other maids and these, I fear, gave my wife in many ways a good deal of trouble at first. Now and then I had to be called in to read the riot act. Dallas Wynne Wilson recalls:

Armistice Day... I think it was the next day, that all our female staff, about ten of them, gave notice in a mass – the soldiers were all going! I think most of them withdrew it afterwards.

The Age of the Cycle

We must pay tribute to the bicycle, which proved such a major instrument of social change in the late nineteenth and early twentieth centuries. It provided mobility at comparatively low cost – a significant factor for the less wealthy.

the reverse of the card read 'Elsie, Irene, May, row). Bessy, Lily, Rose Agnes (Head Dormitory d). Old School House, 8.

From the number of advertisements seen, it is clear that many of Holt's shops stocked cycles, catering for increasing demand. At the eastern end of the Market Place, in the premises vacated by the International Stores, Tower Cycle Stores became established, so-named after their first location, in Shirehall Plain, near the water tower. A newspaper cutting in the family collection reveals that 'Mr AV Shipp moved to Holt after being in the cycle business at Botesdale, near Diss'. This store went on to become the chief outlet for bicycles in Holt for more than fifty years.

se Barrett on her rounds bike and dog.

Holt Cycling Club

In the early days at Holt and, in fact, for a good
many years the only means of getting about was by bicycle.
The Norfolk roads before the war were none too good, but afterwards they were abominably bad.
The road to Cromer was in such a shocking state that I devoted myself to a newspaper campaign
in the Eastern Daily Press, writing a number of derisive and somewhat facetious letters, which were
taken up and supported by many other correspondents. I was so successful in this that for some
time the road was locally known as 'my road'. (Dallas Wynne Wilson)

Kelling
Sanatorium

GRESHAM'S

TEA GARDENS
TO KELLING
and WEYBOURNE

WORKHOUSE LANE

HOLT
OWLS

HOLT HALL

CROMER ROAD

ELSDENS
GARAGE

NORTH
NORFOLK
GARAGE

WHITE
LION
BOWLING
GREEN

PEACOCK LANE

CHAPTER
EIGHT

Laundry

BULL
STREET

THE WHITE LION

WHITE
LION STREET

Chapter 8

White Lion Street

We are standing in the market place, looking north, with the White Lion Hotel at the bottom on the right, trees before and trees behind. The chestnut to the left of the picture is growing on Star Plain, with the Star Inn beyond. There is a wall at the end of the street, and it is just possible to see a pantiled roof beneath the summer foliage. There's a gateway through... to the Quaker Meeting House.

> Opposite the White Lion Hotel was the Quaker Meeting House, with trees before it. It stood back from the road, and was pulled down in the present century, to make room for undistinguished buildings – an act of vandalism which would hardly be allowed now. (Jane Hales, 1967)

This winter view shows the Quaker building more clearly.

Nelson House, (with the porch on the right), gains its name from its association with Nelson's family, who owned it in the early nineteenth century. When the porch roof was undergoing repairs several years ago, the lead used in its construction was found to bear a footprint, as well as the name WB Suckling, and a date, 1828. Suckling is the family name of Nelson's mother. Reputedly, Nelson himself stayed here, and, while in the town, enjoyed a game of bowls on the White Lion Green. Nelson's association with the house is commemorated each year on the anniversary of the Battle of Trafalgar, October 21st. During building work in the 1960s, an old salt-glazed earthenware wine jar was discovered in the garden. It was identified as a bellarmine, and thought to have been made in Freschen, in the Low Countries, in the mid-sixteenth century.

Beyond Nelson House we see iron railings set on a low wall, a driveway and a hedge beyond. This is the entrance to Wansbeck House. The main part of the house is set back from the road, with extensive gardens behind. At one stage, as we have read, this house served as a boarding-house for Gresham's. From this angle it is not possible to see the site of the present Post Office, but the Angel Inn stood there until the 1929, then demolished.

Angel Inn

Approaching the end of an era... We see below Cook's stage-coach on a special journey, as its regular route was Norwich to Cromer, via Roughton, which we can see plainly. Is it the name 'Erpingham' obscured behind the rear wheel? We can see the brick chimney to the brewery, to the left and behind the hotel. This was demolished in the twenties by the building firm of Royall and Jex – a useful supply of bricks! Billy Royall and his wife May ran the White Lion. Mr CW Jex ran everything else! The White Lion was a very popular place at this time, with an long-established bowling-green, and an early base for football teams. The Bowls Club developed into a very strong team in the thirties, in particular.

While on the subject of popular town activities, we should include Scouts and Guides, not forgetting their junior versions. Here is a Scout group from early in the century, with Alec Beith holding the drum, which is still in the family possession.

On the corner where Bull Street runs into White Lion Street, and the start of Cromer Road, was the site of a laundry belonging to the Hallows family.

A Preston photo of Holt people in the Market Place
celebrating the Coronation of George V and Queen Mary.

Coronation Day, Thursday, June 22nd 1911.

The day's programme was as follows: 10.30 am, Divine Services, at the Parish Church and the United Methodist Church. 1pm, general assembly in the Market Place, and proceed to the Sports Ground, Peacock Lane, headed by the band. 1.45pm, general sports. 6pm, children to assemble on the Sports ground, and preceded by the band, march to the Concert Hall. 6.30, Children's tea in the Concert Hall. 8pm, dancing on the Spout Hills. 10pm, close of the Day's Festivities.

Peacock Lane, c1875

Peacock Lane

There was a Peacock Farm here in the nineteenth century, and Jane Hales records that 'it may get its name from one Peter Pecock, who owned land hereabouts in the Middle Ages.' In the early twentieth century there was some housing, mainly on the right-hand side leaving town, and what was called the town's sports ground (but not football pitch, as yet.) The sports event of Holt's 1911 Coronation celebrations took place here, on Thursday, June 22nd 1911.

Midsummer, fine weather… Jane Hales certainly has vivid memories of the day:

> Entertainments and pastimes have changed over the years, but most children would still enjoy a day such as that of the Coronation of King George V in the very hot summer of 1911. I looked forward to it eagerly. I had a 'gold' medal which I wore, but it tarnished to its true constituents and disillusioned me. In the morning I was taken to church, which I had not bargained for. In the afternoon I went to sports in a meadow. What thrilled me the most was 'Tilting the Bucket'. A bucket full of water was suspended. At the bottom of the bucket was a wooden flap with a hole in it. Men with long poles were pulled in open carts beneath the bucket, the object being to pass the pole through the hole and thus escape a ducking. A dirty-looking man was an expert at it, most got soaked. When bedtime came, my mother lit a Chinese lantern outside my bedroom window to celebrate the coronation.

Coronation programme.

Holt Playing Fields Association

The time came for a permanent base for sport in the town, and an association was formed. Here is an account of its progress, taken from a membership card of the period.

In September 1926 the question of a playing-field for Holt was first raised at a meeting of the Parish Council. As a result, a committee was appointed to report on suitable sites, and it was eventually decided that a field in Peacock Lane, belonging to Mr Burcham-Rogers, was the most desirable. At this stage, the Holt Branch of the Playing Fields Association was formed, and having approved the site recommended by the Parish Council, negotiations were commenced with Mr Burcham-Rogers for the purchase of the land. As this was not possible at the time, the Association entered into a contract to hire the land on a long lease with the option of renewal. Fortunately, since then, Mr Burcham-Rogers has expressed his willingness to sell the ground, and within a very short time it will become the property of the Holt Playing Fields

Association. The fact that a Playing Field has become available for Holt is largely due to the activities of Gresham's School and the generosity of its Headmaster, Mr JR Eccles, for, as a result of a Christmas Fair held at the school, no less a sum than £200 was handed over to the Association, while Mr Eccles personally gave a donation of £100.

Two Garages

Earle Kirby tells of the reasons leading to his parents' choice of moving to Holt in 1920. Their story ties in the early history of both of the garages that became established in Cromer Road. Elsdens (now Thurlow Nunn) was founded in the early years of the century, and the North Norfolk Garage (now demolished) in the early twenties. His parents' story does seem particularly redolent of the era.

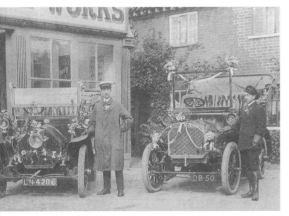

...dding cars at ...g Brothers, later to ...ome North Norfolk ...age.

Earle Kirby "My mother's father had a shop in Peckham High Street; they were doing all right, but then my grandfather got consumption, which I think was pretty rapid. Then my mother's brother – fifteen at the time – caught it as well, and they died within a short time of each other. There was no widow's pension, they didn't know what to do, they had to let the shop go, they ran on hard times. My mother married, in error I think we'd say, had a little girl, my Auntie Win, but everything went wrong. They were in Ipswich by this time, and this is where my mother came to meet the man who was to become my father. Now at that time he had a good job as Company Secretary to a large concern; but having fallen in love with my mother, he was willing to do anything, give up this job and more or less emigrate. He wanted somewhere out of the way but not too far out of the way; in short they needed to get away from my mother's first husband, so he couldn't interfere with the family any more, he was being a big nuisance. In those days you couldn't get about very easily, so father looked in the adverts in the paper, and Elsdens garage were advertising for a Company Secretary – he applied and got the job.

...xury limousine at Elsdens ...rage.

So the family moved up here, he settled in to the job, only to find himself not long after – together with two other employees – getting the sack. My father was up here, with no work or anything at all – but he was dynamic, he wouldn't let anything beat him, he looked

Earle Kirby "Another thing about Holt, and this is when I was in the pram, but my father told me. Early in their time in Holt, my parents decided to visit the sea, so they set off on foot, with a picnic, for Salthouse. They got halfway down Bard Hill, when they began to think better of it – they met a gang of boys, who set about stoning them back up the hill! They had to beat a hasty retreat! When my father later strode up to Holt Police station with a complaint, they calmly told him that it was all quite normal! People in villages were very territorial in those days."

Holt United, 1928–29. back row, left to right; WE Craske (treasurer), Newland, J. Craske, A Broughton, W Long, T Kaye, BH Bond (secretary). Seated, W Budrell, F Ketterham, M King (chairman), H West, (captain), R Walker, G Wright, A Algar, H Weston. This team reached the final of the Norfolk Senior Cup, at the Nest, Norwich, losing 2–1 to Yarmouth Town.

around; they were then selling the old coach establishment of Ling down the road. So father was commissioned by six or seven business people in Holt, including FW Baker, old John Hallows and others, to form the North Norfolk Garage Company Ltd. My father did all the paperwork for them to get it off the ground; and he worked there for thirty-odd years. He was a marvellous book-keeper – he was the only person I know who was able to add pound shillings and pence in three columns – all at once, brilliant."

Holt Owls

Roly High writes:

Holt United Football Club was formed in 1893, and was one of the founder members of the North Norfolk and Norwich League in 1895. By 1927 the teams had won this league five times. They played on the football field opposite Elsdens garage on the Cromer Road. The dressing-rooms were in the White Lion. In 1933, the ground was located on the new playing-field on Jubilee Road. As schoolboys we were asked to pick up stones in preparation for the seeding.

As a lad, Earle Kirby enjoyed the dramas on and off the pitch.

Earle Kirby "When I was old enough to appreciate football, I liked to nip away and go and watch the matches opposite Elsdens garage. I used to craze my parents for money so I could get in the ground. To stop people cheating, the club erected a line of posts to stop people getting a free look, and put sackcloth all the way along. One day I remember very well indeed; inside the field at that stage there was a pond that's since been filled in. Now they were a very violent crowd in those days, and there used to be a saying, 'If they didn't win the game, they'd win the fight afterwards!' Well, Holt did lose that week, and they took it out on the ref – they threw him in the pond! I was there when that happened. There wasn't any disciplinary reaction to that, and I think the ref took it as part of life round here!"

Cromer Road

We are indebted to Jane Hales for some background to housing development here. We should point out that the road now known as Pearsons Road was formerly Workhouse Lane:

> Building along the Cromer Road, beyond the North Norfolk Garage, did not begin until the last two decades of the nineteenth century, apart from a few older houses and cottages. Yew Tree Cottage is old, and Applegarth (formerly California) at the junction of Kelling Road and Pearsons Road. Kenwyn, a Gresham school establishment, was known formerly as Bengal Lodge, and was the home of Robert Rust, who had been a pilot on the Hoogli. In the 1880s, Carlton Terrace was put up Mr Hewitt of Letheringsett. Adjoining was the tea garden and nursery of Mr Rush. The Gresham villas date from 1903. A little further on, on the same side of the road, is a remarkable milestone, bearing the inscription 3$\frac{1}{2}$ furlongs to Holt.

The Tea Gardens

No doubt this was an attractive place to pause if you came to Holt in order to visit sick relatives at the Kelling Sanatorium.

David Stokes "In 1923, my parents bought a market garden from Mr Winn; we sold fruit, vegetables, tomatoes and cut flowers. Previously, Mr Rush had owned it. The Tea Gardens, only part of the property, lay in front on the Cromer Road. These were very attractive, with a greenhouse, pergolas, and flowers. The gardens extended back on to Mr Beresford's land behind, with one part of the boundary being Gresham's school playing fields. The Tea Gardens were open from Whitsun to the end of September. One thing I remember very well is that we made and sold our own ice-cream. The ice man came once a week with a hundredweight of ice, which was placed in a special wooden tub, lined with zinc, and fitted with a handle and beaters. The process was: add a measure of salt, the milk and the cream (half of each), and cochineal colouring, then turn the handle. The beaters got to work – and hey presto, ice-cream!

For our dog, Jason, and myself, the best moment came when they changed over from making strawberry to vanilla ice-cream, and the beaters had to be washed in the sink. If we timed it right, we got to lick the beaters before they were washed and sterilised! Every week we went to Holt Station to collect the gallon of cream we'd ordered, which the dairy sent up. We kept a donkey and cart, which Mother used for shopping. It was great fun growing up there as a child, as there was room to run around and ride a bike in the garden. Ted High was the garden foreman; he lived down Grove Lane, where he kept

View down Cromer Road, with the entrance to the Tea Gardens to the left.

goats in a field, together with our donkey. Reg Cott was the under-gardener, and there was also a boy employed. The Tea Gardens closed in 1932 and we rented Acacias, (now the Lawns), which we ran as a guest house. Mrs Bone was our cook."

Before we come to Gresham's, we'll take a slight detour down Kelling Road, and visit Holt Hall.

Holt Hall

The hall was built in the 1840s, and substantially enlarged about twenty years later. Jane Hales notes (1967) that 'An old hall was on the site of the present cottages, near the lake. There are remains of an ancient chapel here, but they have become even more ruinous of late years.' John Henry Burcham Burcham-Rogers inherited the Holt Hall estate from his father John Rogers in 1906; ownership of the Hall remained with him until his own death in 1945. He attached the 'Burcham' to the front of his own surname Rogers in 1908, by deed poll, so saw out his own days in a double-barrelled guise. In an informative booklet on the Hall's history, Graham Parker says that 'It seems surprising that very little is known of the family except that they appear to have been very stern and class-conscious and were very remote from the rest of Holt society. They were often abroad and also had a property in London. One of the former gardeners from the Hall told of packing large hampers from the kitchen gardens and sending them to London by train. They had their

'HOLT HALL'

family pew in church; servants and tenants were not allowed to walk to church along Church Walk – they had to use a parallel path instead. Typically, Mr Burcham-Rogers was a local magistrate.' None of this paints a very flattering portrait; perhaps we should remember the family's generosity to St Andrew's building fund." (see Chapter Seven)

Fêtes

The Burcham-Rogers family, however, threw open their grounds to hold a Fête, every so often, as did the owners of other large houses. Here Beatrice Scarr (née King) recalls the summer fête of the era:

Fêtes were held in many big country houses and in our rectory too. Quite often we would have to walk a few miles to these or later we could bicycle to them. I well remember those in Holt Hall, Dr Skrimshire's garden, the Lee Warner's home and Sir Alfred Jodrell's at Bayfield Hall, which was particularly interesting as Sir Alfred had peacocks strutting around. He always reminded me of Sir Roger de Coverley: very dignified. He often presented my father with pheasants and partridges. The river Glaven ran through his park and this is where our little stream flowed eventually and thence out into the sea. One of the features was 'walking the greasy pole' over the river. It looked horrible to do and was very rarely achieved. The usual result was a plunge into the rather murky river, but it always attracted a huge crowd and caused much merriment! Fêtes were quite dressy affairs, pretty frocks and large hats to protect one from the sun...

The Lee-Warners, two delightful ladies, lived in a castle-like home and gave their yearly fête in aid of the new Guinea Mission. The tower room was said to be haunted, but Miss Lee Warner told me that she thought this resulted from their having locked it up when they went away and let the house. But she admitted she had seen a little grey lady walking in the garden. But then, with a twinkle in her eye, she thought she must have been suffering from indigestion! The other lady, Miss Chaplin, was a companion. They had a huge revolving musical box which I loved.

The Burcham-Rogers of Holt Hall had more of a garden party than a fête. Sir Burcham we remember particularly because we thought he was a particularly good cheat at croquet! He often seemed to quietly edge his ball into a better position! It was politic to let him win anyhow.

A shot of the new buildings very near completion. How very splendid – imagine their impact on everybody – pupils, parents, staff, townspeople. In the foreground we can see the railway lines laid for construction traffic.

George Howson

Gresham's

George Howson – Visionary

We are now in a position to compare the Holt of 1900 with the Holt of today, and in reflecting on the changes seen, it is clear that so much stems from the vision of one man – George Howson. It was he who was appointed to the post of Head Master by Governors, mainly drawn from members of the Fishmongers Company, to initiate and advance the transformation of The Holt Grammar School of Sir John Gresham into Gresham's. It was he who took over the mantle of the Revd Jolliffe, inheriting his fifty pupils, and, for the first three years of his tenure, the buildings in the Market Place, too. In that time, these new red-brick palaces of learning were rising on farmland down the Cromer Road. Once occupied, and the new institution was taking shape, the number of his pupils rose steadily, year on year, until they topped the two hundred nine years later. An amazing feat.

It has to be said, however, that personal vision was not the only source of this phenomenon. As always with major innovations, external circumstances need to be favourable, and they certainly were for Howson, in more than one way. First, in 1899, revenues of the school increased, by a huge factor, through sharply rising rents from property in London left as an endowment by Sir John Gresham. At much the same time, the Endowment Act was passed in Parliament,

ve Benson George
vson was a man of vision
, at the age of forty,
ed his chance, with full
port from enlightened
rernors, to create a new
ool with a modern
riculum in the heart of
l Norfolk. A bachelor
lded to his school,
vson attracted an able
f in tune with his ideas.
inspired respect rather
n love, set a high moral
e, mesmerised the
ents and within ten years
made his school
onally renowned.
sham's recruited talented
sensitive boys who
ild have sunk without
e at tougher, traditional
lic schools: Reith, Britten,
len, Spender, to name
a few. In January 1919
rge Howson died,
ntally and physically
austed, aged 58.

d Master Howson seated
i his pupils in front of the
ool.

which compelled charitable institutions to spend their monies in worthy ways. Third, the Chairman of the Board of Governors was Sir Edward Busk, Vice-Chancellor of London University; he was a key figure in educational circles at that time, a man determined to see substantial changes take place in the curriculum and management of schools.

I take this background information from Steve Benson's compelling narrative of the school in the twentieth century, *I Will Plant Me a Tree*. I recommend it as an absorbing study of a school in evolution. More particularly, read it for the brilliant analysis of the complex figure of Howson himself, a man who he brings vividly to life. But having briefly sketched in the nature of the development of Gresham's, I need to shift our focus back to the brief for this book – the town itself – and try and identify the effects of this major expansion on its life and its economy. You will recall that Wynne Wilson spoke of the domestic staff employed in his boarding-house. 'We had eight or nine dormitory and other maids…', he counted. Let's take this enumeration further. There were kitchen staff, perhaps three. Each boarding-house had its own gardener, and gardener's boy, who grew produce for the kitchen, an odd-job man, and cleaners. There were separate staff for the housemaster and his family. We've reached at least twelve staff – perhaps fourteen? - per boarding-house, of which there were four by 1911. There were ground staff for the playing-fields, a secretariat, laboratory technicians; there was the CCF, with resident Sergeant-Major. Who have we missed? – the teaching staff! – fourteen by 1908. The totals grow. Nor should we forget the masters who lived in town, who had their own household retinue. Do we approach a hundred? Holt's population in 1900 was 1854, in just over 400 households. Over ten years the number of jobs had hugely increased. Not all, undoubtedly, went to people already

175

resident in Holt. But no doubt most of them spent their money in Holt's shops.

Demonstrably, Holt's economy was given a huge boost by the establishment of its new boarding-school. And money brings money. It is hard to imagine Mr Cubitt Cooke of the Feathers being interested in settling in a town where style went unnoticed; and after all, money nourishes style. His daughters noted that his custom was primarily commercial travellers (visiting a town where there was wealth to be tapped) and the parents of Gresham's pupils, who were no doubt flattered to be met at Holt Station by his special, yellow coach. But I believe there was a further consequence to the sudden supply of jobs in what we would now term the service industry – in terms of stability of the population. Even in the small number of case histories we have seen in the course of this volume, we know that girls, after leaving school at fourteen, usually went into service – often away from their home. With Gresham's on their doorstep, there was a much more local source of work. This made for a more cohesive society, a characteristic which becomes more evident in the late twenties and thirties; it would require the span of a generation to see this effect.

The other clear benefit brought by Gresham's is in the area of cultural life. In their survey of the previous year's events, the Holt Almanacks record many instances of concerts, lectures, recitals, dramatic productions, winter and summer. From these entries it is impossible to determine the numbers attending, but the tone of reporting is always very positive.

Howson's Reforms

There are three aspects to the 'reformist' approach adopted by Howson. The first concerns the curriculum he introduced, where Sciences and Modern Languages were brought to the fore, at the expense of the classics. The following subjects were compulsory: the three 'R's, Geography, History, French, Natural Science, Drawing, Music and Drill. Secondly, games were to be played for exercise and not status; a third feature was that corporal punishment was an occasional, and by no means routine, response to misdemeanours. Gresham's was not the only school to be working along these lines, but it very quickly achieved national prominence for its successes in Oxbridge Scholarships. It attracted parents of the liberal middle-classes, with significant recruitment from politicians, industrialists, liberal intellectuals. Howson quoted the following words with approval in his 1902 Prospectus. 'The training of our schools and colleges must daily become more and more the training for action... for practical purposes. Are there not thousands of lads today plodding away, or supposed to be plodding away, at the ancient classics, who will never make anything of them... Think of the wasted time... entirely wasted as far as available knowledge is concerned...'

JR Eccles

Howson's successor was his long-serving lieutenant, JR Eccles, who took over in 1919. It has to be said that Howson, however effective he was as an educational innovator, left no trace whatsoever in the annals of the town! He features on no committee, no minutes, no report, no anecdote. I have come across no mention of his name whatsoever. Holt gave him his location for a school, but beyond that, it seemed to serve little purpose for himself or his boys, who, during his years, were barred from entry to the town, with prefects posted on sentry duty at key moments! Whether it was an aspect of deliberate policy, or simply personal preference, Eccles, however, took a substantial part in town affairs, and was keen to promote initiatives on behalf of townspeople. We have already met one instance of this in the role he played in the establishment of a playing field.

> When JR Eccles came to Holt with the first batch of masters for the new Gresham school, he took a great fancy to Woodlands, and persuaded the Governors to purchase it as a boarding-house in 1905. Mr Eccles eventually became Headmaster, and did a lot for Holt. A cul de sac off the Cromer Road was named after him. (Jane Hales)

er book *When Heroes* Sue Smart charts the y tragic deaths in the World War of men who been Howson's pupils at sham's. It is a heart-ing account of lives cut t, made all the more nant by their shared and their attachment to school.

Eccles

st physics laboratory – e of the art.

Wystan Hugh Auden, 1907–73, Old Greshamian

WH Auden was a prolific writer, creating one of the richest oeuvres of any poet of the twentieth century. His work is characterised by a sharp, probing wit, accompanied by a profound sense of moral issues. In his poems he can evoke deep pathos, with a particular gift for the love poem. Recently, one of his works, Funeral Blues, found a new audience when it was recited in the 1994 hit film Four Weddings and a Funeral. He attracted controversy, for different reasons, throughout his career, he remains one of the most accomplished and significant writers of his time.

Why do I choose to single out Auden? First, because in the realm of literature, he is the most eminent of them all; and quite interestingly from our point of view, he contributed in the thirties to a collection of essays, 'Old School' whose subject was the contributors' several school experiences. This was edited by Graham Greene. The other reason for the choice of Auden is the fact that his surname is now attached in perpetuity to Gresham's by its theatre. Early in his essay in the collection, entitled Honour (Gresham's School, Holt), he gives a pen-portrait of himself as a youth:

As what one sees depends on what one is, I must begin with a description of myself at that time. The son of book-loving, Anglo-Catholic parents of the professional class, the youngest of three brothers, I was – and in some respects still am – mentally precocious, physically backward, short-sighted, a rabbit at all games, very untidy and grubby, a nail-biter, a physical coward, dishonest, sentimental, with no community sense whatever, in fact a typical little highbrow and difficult child. It says much – perhaps little – for Holt that I was never bullied or molested, I was allowed to make my friends where I chose, and was, taking everything into consideration, very happy throughout my time there. The first condition for a successful school is a beautiful situation and in that respect we were at Holt very fortunate. The school authorities, with extraordinary good sense, set virtually no bounds, a liberty rarely I believe abused. Watching a snow storm come up from the sea over the marshes at Salthouse, and walking in a June dawn (not so legally) by Hempstead Mill are only the two most vivid of a hundred such experiences.

short poem is thought
[h]ave been written by
[Au]en at the age of fifteen
[whil]e he was at Gresham's,
[the] first of his poems he
[cho]se to send home to his
[mot]her. The title defied
[eluc]idation for many years,
[unti]l it was pointed out to
[Aud]en scholars that there is
[a ho]use in Holt, now called
[Hel]egarth, on the corner
[whe]re Pearsons Road meets
[the] Cromer Road, which
[earl]ier in the century bore
[the] name 'California'.

[Cali]fornia

[Th]e twinkling lamps stream
[up t]he hill
[Past] the farm and past the
[...]

[Un]til at the top of the road
[One] sees
[A ro]und moon like a stilton
[che]ese

[A m]an could walk along that
[trac]k
[Fetc]h the moon and bring it
[bac]k
[Or g]ather stars up in his
[han]d
[Like] strawberries on English
[land].

[But] how should I, a poor
[man] dare
[To m]eet so close the full
[mo]on's stare?'
[At] this I stopped and stood
[quit]e still
[The]n turned with quick steps
[dow]n that hill.

[A ne]w classroom. Note the
[orna]te desks.

Having come clean about himself, he feels liberated to speak freely of other aspects of his schooling. He sketches in the curriculum, he commends many staff, of whom he identifies two, 'the two men to whom I owe an immense debt, the master who taught Classics and English, and the Music master.' He offers mordant observations on the genus 'schoolmaster', he applauds the overall sense of fellowship between teacher and taught which he found at Gresham's and which he sees as the best nurture for young minds. He takes issue, however, with the school's 'education of our morals' – the Honour system, analogous to the pledge in Scouting, but adapted to a boarding-school context. In Howson's method, you had both to do the decent thing at all times yourself, but ensure the next chap jolly well did likewise. And if he wouldn't, and your own powers of persuasion in this respect also failed, it was your obligation to tell sir. In essence, he argues it abuses a young adolescent's natural sense of affiliation, turning it into a source of fear. He is quite insistent that this has a damaging effect which can last long into adulthood.

He may, or may not, be right. Perhaps it all depends on the temperament of the adolescent in question. Nor does he allow the necessity for a school to maintain itself through some kind of moral order. The 'Honour' system may not have worked for him; he was, on his own admission, 'mentally precocious', and perhaps he felt its negative aspects rather more keenly than others. A magnified sensibility, after all, is germane to a poet; in respect of the 'moral education' he received at Gresham's, he displays this quality to an extent that is most befitting to his future status in English letters!

Love's Labour's Lost, 1907

Steve Benson Howson's vision encompassed much more than the classroom. Music played a major role in the School's life and he was fortunate to enlist the services of Geoffrey Shaw and later Walter Greatorex as Directors of Music. Weekly recitals by staff and boys became central to the calendar as were periodic orchestral concerts. Music was also essential to the annual Shakespeare play produced in the woods from 1902 onwards which became a major Norfolk event, enhanced by the building of the Open Air Theatre, under the direction of Messrs Spiers and McNeile with boy labour, in 1907. Shaw's incidental music was complemented by EA Robertson's directing skills. Reviews appeared in the national, as well as the local, press.

The chalets were on a turn-
table so they could move
accordingly to the weather.

Kelling Sanatorium

We have just seen the rapid expansion of Gresham's in the
first ten years of the century, and have observed the impact
on the town to which it was attached. Now we come to a
development which took place at exactly the same time, and
which had an equivalent effect on the town. These notes have
been compiled from Dr James Slator's fascinating history of
Kelling Sanatorium, The First Sanitorium for Working Men.

Kelling Sanatorium was founded specifically to handle the
principal illness affecting the nation's health in the late
nineteenth and early twentieth century – tuberculosis of the
lungs. It brought the possibility of fresh-air treatment
otherwise unavailable to the working man. Kelling
Sanatorium was established by Dr H W McConnel, largely
through his involvement with the experiences of his wife
who had developed the disease in 1897, but had recovered
thanks to the intervention of Dr Frederick William Burton
Fanning, a Consultant Physician at Norfolk and Norwich
Hospital. Dr Burton-Fanning ordered fresh-air treatment and
Mrs McConnel recovered, living to an old age.

Dr McConnel was supported in these endeavours by a
wealthy clergyman, the Revd Percey Lloyd, who purchased
Kelling Farm as location for the Sanatorium. This was a

period in which health matters were highly significant at a national level. Information was published in The Times, and money was donated by the Earl and Countess of Leicester, of Holkham Hall, who became Presidents. By 1904, the site was developed to cater for up to forty-two patients, with the building of north and south wards, as well as wooden chalets. The original could house only six patients. By this date, a total of 159 cases had been treated, and these represented forty-eight different trades, from bakers to wood-turners. By 1909, the Sanatorium was well established, with an increase of accommodation, in the form of twenty more single chalets and three double chalets. The Sanatorium was given publicity at the National Association for the Prevention of Tuberculosis exhibition in London, Oxford and Cambridge. This led to a significant increase in donations, most notably from King George V. A year later Queen Mary made a visit, when she agreed to become Patroness of the Sanatorium. By 1913, it consisted of three blocks – the North and South wings for male patients and a women's wing.

Now just a brief description of the treatment. The patient lived in a wooden cubicle as shown in the photo; the cubicle doors were never shut, allowing free entry for wind, rain and snow. It was, after all, known as the fresh-air treatment. The average length of stay was twelve weeks, and patients usually gained about eleven pounds in weight. In subsequent years, methods underwent some changes. For further information, I refer you to Dr Slator's history.

visitors to patients at the
orium.

to Hempstead →

THE LOWES

HOLT STATION

CROWE

EMPSON

STATION ROAD

POLICE STATION

SHRUBLANDS

THE ACACIAS

OLD SCHOOL HOUSE

THE
RAILWAY
HOTEL

CHAPTER
NINE

MARKET
PLACE

Chapter 9

Station Road

The time has come to leave Hol by train. We are still in the Marke Place, by the railings to Old School House, and from here we may just see in the distance the station buildings, the site o which is now by-pass.

We have just left the Railway Hotel to our right, where many clubs and societies held functions.

This was, among other things the headquarters to one of the Homing Pigeon Clubs. We continue our way down the narrow part of Station Road.

J Holmes Randall opened this shop in 1896. Admire the wonderful range of enamel signs on the end wall.

Archie Checkley notes, in his album: 'After working for Mr Randall for fifteen years, Mr EJ Cotts took it over.'

Glancing back at the Market Place we notice the bay windows behind the boys' heads as we do so. How long did they remain?

Parked just outside the gated entrance to Old School House is the Byford delivery cart, with driver 'Squiggles' Norton and Sidney Cook on board.

A few steps on, we turn around for one last, lingering look. We're in 1922 here, and we observe the telegraph poles, with the cables strung aloft; the War Memorial has been in place for about a year. In one of the cobbled cottages to the left lived Arthur Burgess, sign-writer.

Late in 2003 in the early stages of our History Project, Arthur Burgess' grand-daughter, Margaret Hicks, handed me a very old, yellowing newspaper cutting which recorded something very special:

Arthur Burgess – Mirth-maker

Arthur Burgess, sign-writer, with the tools of his trade.

Since he came to Holt in 1921, there has hardly been a social function, dinner or smoking concert, at which Mr Arthur Burgess, of Station Road, Holt, has not delighted the company with his singing. He is popularly known as the Holt Nightingale. Mr Burgess, who is now 66, has always found a joy in singing, and attributes his good health now to the fact that, after being ordered to Norfolk from Lancashire for the benefit of his health, he responded quickly to the Norfolk air, and added affairs of his own as well. He has always been most ready to give his services for any cause, and has sung in fifty villages around Norwich and Yarmouth and North Norfolk. Pigeon club dinners, bowls and football dinners, old folk's parties, fishing club, Post Office dinners and British Legion

Arthur Burgess and friends.

affairs all find a space for Mr Burgess' name on the programme. For who can bridge that dull gap which occurs at times better than this mirth-maker, who by his genial presence, his smile, his splendid voice and pure enunciation is calculated to enliven the most stolid company. While preferring the lighter kind of song, Mr Burgess can always give a song for the occasion. To start with he can sing fifty songs straight through without any help from words or music. He deplores the fact that so many young men nowadays never learn a song through, but when they are called on to sing, have to turn their backs on their audience to see the words on the piano. Mr Burgess was formerly an expert sign-writer, and the face of Holt has benefited from his artistry, for many business firms have employed him to brighten up their premises.

In the summer, with his friends seated on the War Memorial seats, he passes away many an hour singing to their delight. 'The labourer is worthy of his hire, and as an entertainer, Mr Burgess has found the people of Holt most responsive. Although he suffered a severe illness a short while ago, Mr Burgess hopes to go on singing for many years yet, a hope that is endorsed by many of his fellow townsmen.

ellers arriving in Holt by
n would pass this fine
ding on their way into
n.

The Police Station

The red-brick house served as Holt's police station from the time of its building in the middle of the nineteenth century. Our researches to date have yielded nothing on the work of the force, except one small image of a policeman, as pointed out, on page 112. However, we do have an account of a court case, taken from the EDP, which gives a fine picture of one aspect of their tireless pursuit of wrongdoers, particularly in the dark hours, especially when extended tiptoeing is required, and above all, when snooping skills are honed to a fine degree. The Holt Detective Force is in action.

It is eleven o'clock on a dark January night; the scene is the back yard of the Feathers and two members of the force are prowling. We switch to the Shirehall… 'The public part of Holt police court was crowded yesterday for a hearing of a case in which Thomas, Stephen Millgate, owner and licensee of the Feathers Hotel was summoned for supplying intoxicating liquor otherwise than during permitted hours on January, 29th, 1927; and the following were summoned for consuming intoxicating liquor in the same circumstances: Richard Jones, Butcher, Ambrose Bramley, schoolmaster, and one other, Charles William Sly-Jex, manager of Holt Labour Exchange.' We switch back to the Feathers yard. 'PC Banyard stated that at 10.30 pm he was in the yard, saw a light in the bar, and heard voice of men there. Looking through the window, he saw three men standing in front of the counter.' We have to report here that Banyard now held this pose for a full fifteen minutes. 'At 10.45, the landlord turned round with a glass in his hand, drew something from a vessel behind him and

POLICE STATION

Cast your mind back, dear reader, to the affairs of the Board School in New Street, at this time. The new premises in Norwich Road were already under construction, a Headmaster was about to be appointed, Bramley wanted the job...

Was this the very bay window through which PC Banyard espied the landlord serving 'dark liquid' after hours?

stood it on the counter. He also filled another glass with dark liquid. The landlord went to the cash register and the witness (Banyard) heard this ring. One of the men in the bar, whom he afterwards found to be Bramley, drank from the glass containing the dark liquid...' By now reinforcements had arrived in the form of bobby PC Billing, and a tense fourteen minutes, thirty seconds ensued. 'Just before 11pm, witness again saw the landlord draw yellow liquid from a vessel behind him, and fill the glass that had had the dark liquid.' Mixing drinks, too, oh no! 'Witness tried the doors of the hotel but they were locked. 'Immediately after, one of the doors opened and Bramley came outside.' Both bobbies seized their opportunity, forcing an entrance through the open door, and on into the bar, where they found Jex, Jones, and the landlord. 'On the counter stood two glasses, one containing yellow liquid, one containing black liquid and an empty glass.' Banyard and Billing did the heroic thing. 'Witness seized two of the glasses and Billing the other, and tasted and smelled the contents. That near Jex contained neat whiskey.' All incriminating, scene-of-the-crime stuff – and very tasty too.

The account of the next phase gets very involved, with excuses and counter-excuses being bandied at extreme velocity. At issue is the question of the exact minute at which each did – or didn't - lift his glass to consume the contents. 'I have not touched my drink,' said Jex. 'Nor have I!' said Jones. Best is the weedling from the landlord that the men had booked into the hotel as guests! When that failed, he tried another tack – 'These gentlemen are my friends, and I've treated them to a drink.' To no avail.

The case ended with their lawyer making this plea. 'Mr Millgate has a fine record. For twenty-three years, including the war, he served in a cavalry regiment. He was afterwards trained in the management of hotels, and was recently at the Bell Hotel, Norwich for five years. A short while ago he invested the whole of his capital in the purchase of the Feathers Hotel. The three others were also of extremely excellent character. Bramley, a local schoolteacher, had come into the hotel shortly before tea to await a telephone call from Mansfield as to the condition of his mother who was lying seriously ill there. For several nights before and after the 29th Bramley had come into the hotel for that purpose. He was a particular friend of Millgate, both were keen gardeners...'

After some discussion with his colleagues Chairman of the

Bench, Lt Col F Watson-Kennedy announced their verdict – a conviction for Millgate (fined £5), Bramley (fined £1) and Jones (fined £1). Jex walked (scotch)-free!

CW Jex - A Forgotten Unforgettable

Early in the Project, I received a letter from a man alerting me of the role played by his grandfather in Holt, in our period 1900-1930. I made a note of the name, read the article enclosed, scanned the photos inside his envelope and carried on with the job in hand. The task of looking out for mention of grandfather's name was made easier by its singularity – Sly-Jex (in full), Jex for short. However, it has to be said that probably six months passed before I noticed the name again. One of the factors here is the sheer quantity of material perused, of all kinds. However, as I grew more familiar with the names and personalities of the town, Jex began to feature. Indeed, as we have been making our way through the town in these pages, I have brought it to your notice.

Step forward David Sly-Jex, grandson:

It is time to introduce a man who had a powerful influence on Holt during, particularly, the 1920s. This influence extended, in ever-diminishing form, to Norfolk county and also nationally. Charles William Sly-Jex lived in Holt until his early death in 1932. His mother was Amelia Sly-Jex but there were some doubts about the identity of his father, encouraging the creation of a number of outrageous rumours. He grew to fulfil a number of significant roles. After being apprenticed to a butcher he opened his own shop. He became a leading, indeed a national figure with the British Legion in addition to his Holt and East Anglian responsibilities, created the first Labour Exchange for Holt, was a partner in a local building company, was a member of Holt Parish Council, Chairman, respectively, of Holt Fire Brigade, Football Club, Workingmen's Club, Pigeon Club; at the time of his death he was in the chair of Iona Lodge Norfolk Druidic Circle, as well as being a prominent member of the Silver Owl Lodge of Buffaloes! He served with the RASC in Palestine in World War One, and returned home with the seed of a monkey-puzzle tree which he planted in the front garden of his home in Kelling Road. He called the house 'Ramleh' which was named after Ramallah in Palestine, but he had never been told how it should be spelt! After the war he interested himself in the ex-servicemen's movement which eventually came to be called the British Legion. In addition to chairing the Holt branch, he held a wide number of posts throughout the Legion, including membership of the East Anglia Area Council as well as serving

Jex

...ther of the enterprises of ...Jex.

...**nn Turner** "He was a ...racter all right, he did ...olutely everything, and ...was one step ahead of ...m all. He was a very ...pular man, except with ...se who were jealous of ...1; that was a very serious ...ng in those days, much ...rse than it is now. He did ...awful lot to help other ...ople as well, he was ...ways there. He went at the ...ible all the time, he went ...ooting up the street, with ...etermined look about ...1, as if he was heading ...newhere and didn't have ...' time to spare…"

on the National Executive Council; there his role was to represent the Other Ranks or Non-Commissioned Officers. A number of generals also served on this council, so before each meeting in London, my grandfather would carefully place a packet of five Woodbine cigarettes in his top pocket. Every time he produced it at the meetings they would say, 'Put that away, Jex!' – and hand out the cigars. He always returned with a pocket full of them, including the occasional Cuban luxury which gave him a great deal of pleasure.

The Railway

Holt's railway dates from 1884, thanks to the ambitions of the Eastern and Midlands Railway, which later became and Midland and Great Northern Railway Company (the M&GN).

We see above the original station, which burnt down in 1926, to be replaced by the building below.

The nearest station down the line was Melton Constable, where there was a connection with the Lynn-Yarmouth line; your journey then took you through the following places: Hindolveston, Guestwick, Whitwell and Reepham, Lenwade, Attlebridge, Drayton, Hellesdon and on to Norwich City Station. In the other direction, you could travel to Weybourne, Sheringham and Cromer, from 1887, where there were links with the Great Eastern. By the time we enter 1900, the railway service was well-set and fully integrated into the life of the town. This was a key factor in Holt's development in the twentieth century. We have already seen the founding and rapid growth of two major initiatives down the Cromer Road in the early 1900s, and neither would ever have been successful if a rail network had not already been established. However committed Dr McConnel was to the fresh-air treatment for consumption, his Kelling Sanatorium would have quite simply lacked patients without an accessible means of travel; and however visionary Howson and his

is was the kiosk on the
tform, constructed of
oden planks. Already the
ior porter has his
istcoat, with watch and
ain, but he is fast growing
t of his uniform! It is
rth noting that the
tional railway network led
time being centralised
oughout Britain.

e poster is one of the few
ginals commissioned by
e Midland and Great
rthern Railway.

Governors were, their school would have been bare of boarders – and therefore, no Public School – without the train connections to all parts of the country. The railway's impact on the structure of agriculture in the region was, of course, extensive, and provided a staple portion of its trade, including livestock for the Friday market. As regards direct impact on commerce in the town, however, its effect was less. We may speculate that Charles Winn would not have bought the land to develop his nursery in New Street without the MG&N, as he was dependent on regular and reliable contact with Covent Garden. It is fair to surmise that Alfred Lee's liquor business expanded with the availability of goods brought in by train.

Undoubtedly, however, the most profound change to Holt came in the form of a business which in the course of the century would eclipse all others – the holidaymaker.

But we should not overlook Holt station itself as a having a rich contribution to the life of the town, in terms of the employment opportunities it brought. I am grateful to Ian Hurst, former Director of the North Norfolk Railway, and lifelong student of the rail network in Britain, for his illuminating discourse.

He started by outlining the personnel required to man the service.

Ian Hurst 'The M&GN line through Holt handled both passenger and goods traffic, and in order to run the whole operation, a considerable workforce was required. At the station itself, there would have been porters, booking clerks, and of course the station master, who was a respected figure in the town. And don't forget, a degree of comfort and a warm welcome (literally, a coal fire in the waiting-room!) was expected by the travelling public. The station staff took a pride in their job, keeping everywhere – including the station garden – in good order. There was a level crossing and a signal box, with as many as four signalmen to cover different shifts and sickness, with relief staff probably provided from Melton Constable. Clerks were needed to check goods in and out of the goods yard, and drivers had to shunt the rolling-stock. We shouldn't forget the carters working there, nor the draymen, perhaps two. In addition, there was a special traffic at Holt because of the quarry down the line - the stone pits – that would have attracted further people, loading and checking the wagons. Then we move on to the maintenance gang; here we would count at least eight people - the ganger and his men who were responsible for a section of track to look after – perhaps four or five miles in extent; each station had its own gang to care for the section of track up to roughly the halfway point to the next station. Their jobs would consist of cutting down trees, clearing weeds, tightening the bolts on the track, checking the ballast and the general safety of the whole outfit – quite a major operation. In the early years of the century, the workforce was almost entirely male; there might have been one or two women in the booking office. In total, we must be approaching the forty to fifty mark.'

Ian goes on to talk about the employment conditions that pertained.

A train is coming in; the pony and cart have to wait.

Note the former granary building belonging to Page and Turner (now Thaxters) in the goods yard, and the very tall signal-box behind.

11th January 1924. The second annual dinner organised by the railway workers employed at Holt station took place at the Shirehall, when the indoor and outdoor staffs, to the number of fifty, sat down to a dinner catered for by Mr G Platten. An enjoyable evening was spent, Mr WJ Munson (station master) occupying the chair.

"There was something of a family hierarchy, and family connections played a big part - if your dad was on the railway, you often joined yourself. The railway was seen as a steady job for life; the pay was mediocre, but at least you had work; there was a pension fund; on the whole, the railways were good employers. The post of station-master was a graded one – if you performed well in Holt, you would be moved to a larger station down the line. Although Holt, in 1884, was relatively late in getting its rail connection, traditions in the railway industry had become well established by that date. As the Midland Railway and the Great Northern Railway were already large companies, their formation of The Midland and Great Northern brought considerable experience into the venture."

Ian outlines the nature of the traffic through Holt.

"Melton Constable station opened in 1882 as a station on the Lynn–Norwich line, which opened in 1883. It was also the junction for the 1883 line to North Walsham and Yarmouth, with the branch to Holt completed in 1884. Holt was actually a terminus for a while, until the section of line over Kelling Heath to Sheringham and ultimately Cromer was completed in 1887.

From the outset there was a mixture of passenger and freight traffic. One of the famous services was the Leicester Express, which brought in holiday passengers from Midlands cities, and split at Melton Constable; it had portions for Norwich and Yarmouth, and one for Cromer, stopping at Holt. Freight traffic was, of course, two-way, in and out. The 'imports' were primarily coal and products serving the agricultural industry, such as fertiliser. 'Exports' would have been grain, sugar beet, general parcels. And we shouldn't forget the key

A wry view of Holt railway on this postcard.

...Lord We went to our ...rding-school in Norwich ...he train, and we were put ...he charge of the guard; we ...ght a return ticket and ...t the other half for coming ...ne at half-term. And then ...he other end there would ... cab - a horse and cart ... - to meet us at City ...tion. We picked up one or ... girls along the way, at ...yton and Attlebridge, ...ton Constable – there was ...ays about three-quarters ...n hour's wait at Melton ...stable!

...ry Cubitt I went to ...rding-school, and I hated ...ng back and leaving ...rfolk, and I'd hide when it ...s time for me to be ...ching the train, and Aunty ...el used to phone the train ...d ask them to hold it up. ...d they did, you know, ...il I got up there.

...nry Hobart I used to like ...ctical jokes, you know. At ...e time Empson and old ...we both had Belsize ...is, old-fashioned taxis ...h great big brass lamps, ...y used to go up to Holt ...lway Station to wait for ... people, and they'd park ...d to end in front of the ...tion and wait for the train. ...th men went on the ...tform, of course – and a ...end and I had an idea, we ...w the two old cars there, ... tied the cars together – ...ere was a fearful row ...veloped, we had to leave ...ickly!

role played by the railway in bringing in livestock for the Friday market behind the Feathers Hotel.

The extent of the traffic was dictated by the fact that it was a single track line; by July, 1911, there were ten passenger trains each way, three or four goods trains, plus one or two holiday extras in the season."

Were there any significant changes between 1900 and 1930?

"The heyday of the railways was the period leading up to the First World War. As regards the evolution of goods transport, the war did two things; first, it stimulated the development of the lorry; and second, once the conflict was over, the military had lorries in surplus to sell off to enterprising individuals – the start of the road haulage industry. It has to be said that, progressively, profitability decreased throughout the twenties, and by the 1930s, railways were uneconomic in rural areas."

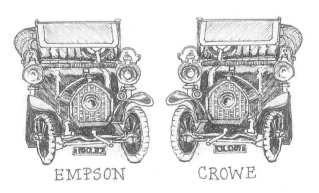

EMPSON   CROWE

The Lowes

We have now crossed over the line at the level crossing, and continued along the Hempstead Road, where on our right we come to the town's second area of common land. My thanks go to Simon Harrap, current Honorary Secretary to the Holt Lowes Trustees, for providing the necessary background information.

The Lowes, an area of heathland amounting to 128 acres to the south of the town, was set aside as a 'poors allotment' by the Enclosure Act of 1807. The owners and occupiers of houses which did not exceed £10 per annum in annual rent had grazing rights for one head of cattle or oxen, or for one gelding or mare; they also had the right to take flag, ling, brakes and furze, for use in their home. Wood and gorse fired ovens, heather made brooms, and bracken was used for bedding. In addition, sand, gravel and flints were building materials. All this was subject to the direction and control of the Trustees, a body consisting of the Rector, churchwardens, guardian of the workhouse and overseers of the poor. However, it is likely that in practice the right to graze was seldom exercised by the people of Holt, both because the land is extremely poor, and also because of its location at some distance from the town.

Footpath on the Lowes.

The advent of cheap coal by rail effectively brought to an end any economic exploitation of the Lowes, and by the end of the 19th century, the area was largely used for recreation. As a consequence, its heathland was already undergoing invasion by pine by the 1880s. This is clear from the first edition of the six inch to 1 mile OS Map, surveyed in 1885 and published in 1886, which shows heathland, with scattered pines marked over almost the whole area. One additional factor which has influenced the Lowes is military activity. During the 1914-1918 war the area was taken over for training purposes.

Jane Hales' diary

I have chosen to end our exploration of Holt with excerpts from a diary kept by Jane Hales as a thirteen-year old, in 1917. It covers a period between May and September, with gaps. It was often hot that summer, and we find many references to the war. Otherwise, this is a very straightforward document, but that in itself is both appealing and revealing. It shows that the 'ordinary' of 1917 was very different from that of today. Jane was clearly in tune with the natural world, and the Holt of those years enjoyed a very intimate link between town and countryside; farmland was just beyond the fringes,animals

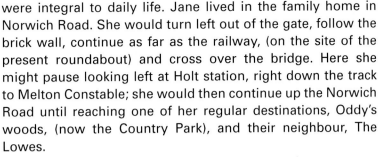

were integral to daily life. Jane lived in the family home in Norwich Road. She would turn left out of the gate, follow the brick wall, continue as far as the railway, (on the site of the present roundabout) and cross over the bridge. Here she might pause looking left at Holt station, right down the track to Melton Constable; she would then continue up the Norwich Road until reaching one of her regular destinations, Oddy's woods, (now the Country Park), and their neighbour, The Lowes.

Monday May 11th Got up fairly early to feed sitting hens. Got out an awfully hot day. Thought Oddy's woods on fire and went up with Mother to see but it was only the Lowes. Lots of trees cut down to stop fire.

Sunday May 13th Went to Letheringsett church with Mother in pony and cart. In afternoon was going to Oddy's woods to read. After tea saw Oddy's woods on fire, went in. Awful smoke, smell is awful at home.

Tuesday May 22nd Warm day but rained off and on. Dug piece of ground for potatoes in morning behind bed by wall in kitchen garden. In afternoon weeded piece of ground that I had not dug the day before and forked over. After tea went up Chapel right up to pinnacle on a ladder. Ripping view.

Wednesday May 23rd Lovely day. Awful smoke along the road. Found we had quite run out of coal so went to get some. About ten in the evening I was awakened by shouting and a fearful fire. I watched from Mother's window. It lit everything up. I went up to the attic and by the light you could see miles around. It was Ellis' stack, and the fire engine was there; we could hear it pumping. I went to bed and heard the clock strike one. I could not have been asleep long when sister was woken by a Zep. She heard a lot of bombs drop. Good thing fire was out. Wonder what spy did it. Awfully sorry missed it.

Thursday May 24th Got up fairly early and went to Ellis' for some eggs. Fire engine still there and stack still smoking. Zeps at Massingham and dropped several bombs but only killed one man and a few horses.

Saturday May 26th Took teas onto Oddy's wood with Mother and had it by statue on path going down straight from arch.

Tuesday May 29th Dull morning but got out lovely day. In afternoon went to Stody common on bikes with Eva and found a place where there was a cliff with thousands of sand martins' nests, but they were too deep to find eggs. Saw a yellow hammer's nest with young bird and egg. Went for tea in field on road from Hunworth to Edgefield. Lovely bit of bog running from road to Lowes. Saw a snipe I think and found some buckweed.

Henry was Jane's elder brother, home on leave from war service.

Thursday May 31st Ripping day. Got up early. Henry has brought home butterflies he caught himself. Gardened before breakfast and in afternoon went fishing with Henry to Thornage. Went to sleep in Henry's room and he in mine.

Friday June 15th Saw three aeroplanes flying in a wedge about eight o'clock. In afternoon helped to put up strawberry nets and watered. Pig was over last night. (*probably the Pulham Pig – Britain's answer to the Zeppelins*)

Wednesday June 20th After tea, Katherine came and we rode into Selbrigg woods. Saw a stack of reeds. Thought they might be for pony litter.

Friday June 22nd Went fishing in afternoon. Trout rising under bridge. Saw airship awfully low flying white ensign and Union Jack. Looked very funny.

Monday June 25th Got up early and went into Oddy's woods. Beautiful morning. Wood glorious. Saw a fritillary butterfly. Biked and came home Hempstead way.

Tuesday July 3rd Got up early and went into Oddy's wood. Ripping. Got a lot of heather.

Wednesday July 4th In afternoon went with Eva in pony cart to Holt Hall to get some strawberries. Watched aeroplanes going in and out of clouds.

Saturday July 14th Beautiful day. In the afternoon went by Pretty Corner to Overstrand in car with Mother, Daddy, sister and Aunt Mabel. We walked from Cromer along the sand to Overstrand. Could not get up the cliffs owing to wire entanglements.

Monday September 3rd Went with Henry to Blakeney marshes and walked on opposite side to Point as far as Morston channel. Walked in all about twelve miles. Mud awful. Sunk to above my knees.

Eva was Jane's governess.

Monday September 17th Eva came and I did a few lessons. Got a load of bracken from the Lowes in morning and then put it out to dry in the yard.

Saturday September 22nd Stayed at the Manor House Hotel at Caister for the night. Electric light in every imaginable place in my room.

Thursday September 27th When cleaning surgery fireplace a pigeon fell on to Mrs Jacobs. It was a carrier and was ringed. Daddy told the police about it and they said it was registered and must be let loose.

Epilogue

We reach the end of our tour. We have seen as much of the town as our current researches allow, but perhaps two hundred pages are quite enough for a first visit. As we journeyed, I found myself reflecting on the sights and sounds, the events, the people, the places. I was very struck by two chance remarks of Gresham's housemaster, Dallas Wynne Wilson. In talking about his cricketing exploits on the field behind Old School House, he said, 'This wall on half-holiday afternoons was lined with idlers from the village.' Then, as war came to Holt, he reported, 'One morning we woke up to find the village market place in front of my house full of soldiers.' Did he really say 'village', twice? He did. I am reminded here of the words of White's Directory, 1845: 'Holt is a neat market town, pleasantly situated on a rising ground, at the junction of several public roads.' ... From its high situation it is remarkably clean and salubrious... there are neat houses in Withers Street.' We find 'neat' repeated twice, too.

Perhaps the key to the appeal – and the heart - of Holt is that its centre is very compact, very intricate. It occupies the space of a village but boasts the attributes of a town. I very much hope that the principal features of Holt in the early twentieth century are more familiar to you now than at the moment you first opened this book.

Acknowledgements

This volume has been produced by Brick Kiln Books,
in association with the Holt History Project.

Brick Kiln Books

Keith Entwistle
Geraldine Entwistle
Technical Advisor – Joshua Dyball
Research assistant – Oscar Newson

Holt History Project

Chairman: Robin Hunt
(Chairman, Chamber of Commerce)
Vice-Chairman: Chris Harrison
(Vice-Chairman, Chamber of Commerce)
Treasurer: Jean Corbett-Jarvis
(Holt Town Council)
Project Consultant: Steve Benson
(Chairman, Holt Society)
Committee: Mike Blair, Paul Brooke, Beryl Griffiths,
Howard Heathfield, Philip High (Chairman, Holt Town
Council), Jane Hunt, Fiona Jolliffe, Terry Thacker,
Mary Wright.

We would like to thank the **Norfolk
Record Office** for permission to
reproduce images from the Checkley
Collection in their custody. We are very
grateful for the help and advice received
from archivists and conservators at the
NRO.

Our thanks go also to: Mrs Mary Butcher,
Mrs Patricia Buxton, Mrs Elsie Checkley,
Mrs A Anderson (niece to Jane Hales),
the Holt Society, Gresham's School, the
family of Dallas Wynne Wilson for their
permission to use material in their
ownership.

We are particularly grateful to Gerald
Cubitt, Lynne Hurst and Peter Mills for
lending images from their collections for
use in this volume.

*Brick Kiln Books and The Holt History Project wish to thank the many people who helped with their
research for this book. We list below those who gave interviews, documents, photographs, postcards,
memories, advice or facilities. We apologise to anyone that we may have inadvetently missed: everyone's
contribution was vital.*

Doreen Abrahams	David Durst	Dora Hills	Mary McGolrick	Derek Salmon
Mary Alexander	Wendy Elsden	Henry Hobart	Mary Morse	Beatrice Scarr
Anthony Baker	Lyn Fairchild	Holt History Group	Peter Moulton	Siddalls Shoes
Michael Baker	Feathers Hotel	Arthur Hopper	Peter Newson	David Sly-Jex
Brian Barrett	Laura Filby	Ian Hurst	Daphne Nichols	Jan Slater
David Bartle	Archie Fuller	Jackdaw Books	Frank Olby	James Slator
Gillian Barwick	Eleanor Finn	John R Jarvis	Brian Payne	John Smart
Joyce Belding	Peter Gillam	John S Jarvis	Picturecraft	Sue Smart
Betty's	Mabel Gotts	Billy Jenkinson	Joan Pointer	Joan Stevens
Bircham Gallery	Malcolm Griffiths	Roger Johnson	Edith Pointin	David Stokes
Ann Brewster	John Hardingham	Mary Jones	Ethel Potter	Brian Thacker
Jumbo Burroughes	Chris Hardingham	Richard Jones	Jack Read	Ann Thompson
John Cardinal	Simon Harrap	Susan Jones	Molly Rich	John Turner
Caroline Carter	Lady Harrod	Earle Kirby	Ivan Riches	Clifford Watts
Harold Cooke	Margaret Hicks	Beryl Knowles	Betty Ringer	Joy Wright
Bridget Cuthbert	Dorothy High	Neville Lee	Tony Ringer	Susan Wharfe
John Craske	Roly High	Brenda Loades	George Rudd	Mary Whitmore
Pauline Cubitt	High Kelling Post Office	Eva Lord	Ruby Rudd	Jimmy Williamson
Mike Curtis	Michael Hill	Betty Mann	Sam Rudd	John Williamson
David Daniels	Adrian Hill	Margot Matthews	Pat Rump	Thea Wortley

Sources

Elizabeth Bellamy – History of Methodism in Holt
Steve Benson – I Will Plant Me a Tree (with Martin Crossley Evans)
Peter Brooks – Holt, Georgian Market Town
Val Fiddian - Salthouse, Story of a Norfolk Village
Jane Hales – Three Centuries of Holt, Ninety Years in One House
   and other titles.

Holt and District – Rhoda Bunn
Lewis Radford - History of Holt
TD Savory – Holt Bench of Magistrates
Sue Smart – When Heroes Die
Dr James Slator – Kelling Hospital
Neil Storey – Norfolk at War
Eastern Daily Press

NB Those quotations in the text set inside inverted commas derive from conversation.
Otherwise, they have been taken from a written source.